# SHROPSHIRE
## PLACE NAMES

### ANTHONY POULTON-SMITH

First published 2009

The History Press
The Mill, Brimscombe Port
Stroud, Gloucestershire, GL5 2QG
www.thehistorypress.co.uk

British Library Cataloguing in Publication Data.
A catalogue record for this book is available from the British Library.

ISBN 978 0 7524 4889 3

Typesetting and origination by The History Press
Printed in Great Britain

# Contents

# Introduction

Shropshire's place names reflect the history, the landscape, and the people of the county. As with Herefordshire to the south, there have been a number of influences from neighbouring Wales, due more to those who relocated here than any constantly changing boundaries. As with other English counties the vast majority of places are Saxon or Old English, with less influence by the Scandinavian tongues this far west.

Roman influences in names are minimal. Celtic names are mainly confined to hills and rivers and are only defined by our knowledge of the modern equivalents such as Welsh, Cornish and Breton. Roads in the county tend to be named for their destination or point of origin, lanes come from the locality, early streets from the developers and residents and modern housing estates have reverted to field names. Pub names are different and require special consideration.

In order to find the meaning of any name, it is important to find as many records which are as old as possible – the earlier the form, the closer to the original uncorrupted form we get, and therefore it becomes easier to define. We should be careful when examining ancient documents for they are not original but simply handwritten copies, and each time a copy is made it is increasingly likely that errors will creep in.

The document which comes instantly to mind is Domesday. When it comes to proper names, this is notoriously unreliable. The great tome is the result of the defeated Saxons, who spoke a Germanic tongue, communicating with the Norman French overlords who used a Latin language. Without a common language, and not being particularly friendly towards each other, it is not surprising that errors in spelling and pronunciation are common. The other information in the book is likely to have been quite correct, for the numerical system is common to both cultures and, other than the proper nouns, there are very few words in the great work. For comparison look at the differences in the English spoken in North America and on this side of the Atlantic which are the same language, while Domesday was produced by two completely different branches of an ancient tongue.

Historically the names of public houses rely heavily on the imagery on the sign. Thus examine the evolution of the pub sign and it goes a long way to showing the development of pub names. The earliest were simply sheaves of barley, a major brewing ingredient, tied to a post or tree (the ale stake) outside a farm or wayside refreshment stop. In later years many differing signs were utilised to tempt customers inside – the tree itself or other local landmark, political allegiance, patriotism, a well-known figure, religion, the monarchy, and coats of arms. The latter could be of the landowners, or a trade associated with the clientele and/or innkeeper. Because of the intricacy of these arms, often just one element was chosen, which is why there are so many oddly coloured animals used as pub names – such as the Red Lion, the most common pub name in the country with over six hundred examples.

Many groups, organisations and individuals have helped in producing this book. Thanks go to the county libraries, Shropshire Archives, many local history groups, Peter Brown of Market Drayton's delightful museum and the publicans who related anecdotal material to relate the beginnings of some truly inventive pub names.

# A

## Abdon

Only two early forms of this name are relevant in defining the origins, as *Abetune* in 1086 and as *Abbeton* in 1227. Undoubtedly this is the Old English or Saxon *tun* preceded by a personal name and is 'the farmstead of a man called Abba'.

One local name is **Earnstrey**, where either Old English *earn treo* or even *earn leah* could have evolved to give the modern form with an identical meaning. The *earn* refers to an eagle, in this case most likely the white-tailed fish eagle. This bird of prey was seen during Roman and Saxon times, nesting as high as possible in the tallest tree at the edge of the forest or clearing; hence why both origins are equally plausible.

Glance at the map and you will see **Monkey's Fold**, not referring to simians but used to describe young hares. There is also **Ploughsters** which comes from *pleg stow* and is nothing to do with farming but was the 'sports place'. Conversely **Four Yokings** does refer to agriculture and is a local term for the area covered during 'a day's ploughing'.

## Acton Burnell

The first part is a very common place name element, hence the reason it is nearly always found with a second element to differentiate. That there are so many Actons is as much because there are three differing origins for the basic name. Here we are unsure if this is the more common 'the farmstead by the oak trees', or if it is 'a specialised farm working oak timber'. What we are sure of is that the addition refers to the Burnell family who were lords of the manor from at least the end of the twelfth century as evidenced by the records of *Actune* in 1086 and *Akton Burnell* in 1198.

*The still-imposing remains of Acton Burnell Castle.*

# Acton Pigott

Listed in Domesday as *Aectune* and in 1242 as *Acton Picot*, the second element refers to the Picot family who were lords of this manor from at least that year. As with the previous entry of Acton Burnell, it is uncertain if this common basic name is 'the farmstead by the oak trees' or 'the farm where oak timbers are worked'.

# Acton Reynald

Another *ac tun* or 'oak tree farmstead', this time the addition of the family name is better documented. The first reference to the family as part of the place name dates from 1416 as *Acton Reigner*. This is rather unusual for the addition is not a family name but a Christian name. The family in question were recorded as de Acton, three of whom had the first name Reyner, the first being here by 1195.

Around this region is found **Boarpit Rough**. On an eighteenth-century map this name is given to a wood alongside an area divided into strips. The name refers to this and describes open field segments.

# Acton Round

Listed in Domesday as *Achetune* and as *Acton la Runde* in 1284, the basic name can be defined yet again as 'the farmstead by the oak trees' or 'farm working oak timbers'. However, the second element is a little more confusing.

It is tempting to suggest this is an early example of the Middle English word *rond* literally referring to the shape of the settlement. However, the record does seem a little early to have Middle English origins, and as the land was held by the Earls of Arundel by this time, 'Arundel' could well have been mistakenly misinterpreted as 'round'.

## Acton Scott

Once again 'the farmstead by the oak trees', unless it was where timbers were worked, as evidenced by the early forms of *Actune* in 1086 and *Scottes Acton* in 1289.

Again the addition refers to the manorial lords, in this case the Scot family who were here in the thirteenth century.

Within the parish is **Alcaston** or 'Alhmund's farmstead', the oddly named **Boss Patch**, which is from *bos* and speaks of 'the stall for cows', and **Potato Plock** which seems to have had two uses for the two elements speak of different things; obviously for the growing of potatoes and also as a sports ground – the likelihood is that these were at different times, although it is possible that these were seasonal differences.

*Fingerpost at Acton Scott.*

## Adderley

Recorded as *Eldredelei* in 1086, *Aldrideleye* in 1283, and as *Addredeleye* in 1284, this comes from a female personal name, unusual although by no means unheard of. Suffixed by the Old English *leah* this is '(place at) the woodland clearing of a woman called Althryth'.

## Adeney

The previous entry was cited as being unusual in that it had its origins in the name of a woman. As if to disprove the rarity of such, here is another. Found as *Eduney* in 1212, *Edeweny* in 1292, and *Addeney* in 1327, this was 'the island of a woman called Eadwynn'. In this instance the term 'island', from Old English *eg*, is used to describe dry ground in marshland.

# Alberbury

Domesday lists this place as *Alberberie*, while the modern form is recorded as early as 1242. Even more remarkable is the fact that this is the third Shropshire place name in a row (alphabetically) to have its origins in a female personal name. This is 'the stronghold of a woman called Aluburh', the suffix from Saxon *burh*.

Occasionally this is also recorded as **Llanfihangel**, which is its Welsh name and refers to the 'church to St Michael' dedication.

*An ancient spring serving Alberbury, today bricked and piped.*

# Albrighton

There are actually two places in the county of Shropshire with this name. This is unusual for two reasons. Firstly it is not a particularly common name, indeed these are the only two places of any size. Thus the second assumption would be that they are in some way related. In fact not only are they quite separate, but have two different origins.

One Albrighton is near Shifnal. Recorded as *Albricstone* in 1086 and *Albrictona* in 1167, this comes form the Saxon for 'the farmstead of Aethelbeorht'. However, the second Albrighton is near Shrewsbury and the Domesday entry of *Etbritone* is very different to that of its modern namesake. It shows that this was a different Saxon personal name and is 'the farmstead of Eadbeorht'.

Within this parish is **Plex Farm**, not a family name but from Middle English *plek* or 'small piece of ground'. Thus we can deduce that the region described was originally much smaller. Indeed this is probably an example of a field name which was later taken for the whole farm. There is also **Pigeon's Rough**, a minor name recalling the former residence or holding by the Pidgeon family who were here from 1691 to 1728.

Nearby are two small hamlets, sharing a common name from the Saxon meaning 'Wiglaf's cottages'. The difference between **Great Wollascott** and **Little Wollascott** does not seem to be size but a question of height.

## Alcaston

Early records of this name are limited to *Aelmundestune* in 1086 and *Alghamston* in 1327. This is another Saxon name from 'the farmstead of a man called Ealhmund'.

## Alderton

Only one listing of note for this name, that of *Olreton* in 1309. Despite this we can be certain that this is not a personal name (as with Aldertons elsewhere), but comes from Old English *alor* + *tun* meaning 'farmstead where alders grow'.

## Alkington

Listed as *Alchetune* in 1086 and *Alkinton* in 1256, this is clearly a Saxon personal name followed by the elements *ing* and *tun*. Therefore we can see this to be from 'the farmstead of the followers or people of Ealha'.

## Alkmund Park

The basic name here comes from Old English *eald mere*. Listed as *Aldemere* in 1291, it is 'the old pond'. Clearly the name was later used to describe a hunting park, although today the name is only used for **Alkmund Park Pool**, where the stretch of water is mentioned twice.

Within this region we also find **Berwick**, from Old English *berewic* 'the outlying grange', and with the same meaning **Little Berwick**, with the addition an obvious one. **Newton** has obvious origins in 'the new settlement', although it has not been 'new' since 1271 at least!

**Laundry Terrace**, **Laundry Cottage** and **Laundry Plantation** are in such close proximity they probably only have one actual origin, the others being transferred names. It is likely the first name was that of the cottage, where washing was taken in. Less obvious is the interestingly named **Ell Hole**, which refers to a right-angled bend in the Severn approaching Leaton Knolls.

## All Stretton

Listed in Domesday as *Aluredestretton*, this is from the Saxon *straet* + *tun* meaning 'the farmstead on the Roman road'. The addition is to differentiate from Church Stretton, referring to an early owner called Alfred.

Locally we find names such as **Botvyle** or 'Botta's woodland clearing'; **Dudgeley**, a name meaning 'Dudd's woodland clearing'; **Prestley**, 'the *leah* or clearing of the priests'; and **Gogbatch**, 'the bog at the boundary stream'. **Naver's Hill** is a combination of Middle English *atten* and Old English *ofer* and telling of 'the place at the flat-topped ridge'. There is also the 'remoteness' name, a laughingly christened place at the furthest extremity of a parish, here given the name **Pensylvania** – pity they got the spelling wrong!

The name of **Top Darnford** may not seem particularly outstanding, yet it conveys more information than its three syllables would appear possible. Firstly there must have been two Darnfords at some time, otherwise it would not have the defining 'higher' beginning. The main name comes from Old English *derne ford* and tells us this was 'the secret ford', not a ford in the obvious sense but a causeway (through a marsh or bog), known to only very few.

Another revealing water name is that of **Quaking Brook**. Listed as *Pontem Trementem* in 1203 and *Le Quakinggebrugge* in 1254 these names speak not of the brook but 'the quaking bridge'. This is much easier to see as a rickety and probably unsafe way to cross the stream which later took the name of the bridge.

The name of **Caer Caradoc** has a first element which is clearly Welsh, *caer* speaking of the 'fort'. The second element would point to the British leader Caratacus, who was defeated by the Romans in AD 51. It is uncertain if this was his stronghold but, if it was, he also gave his name to **Little Caradoc** too.

The local here is the **Yew Tree Inn**. Since pre-Roman times the yew has been venerated by non-Christian religions. It was encouraged to grow in churchyards as it is poisonous and long-lived, useful when there was no wall around the church meant it was open to grazers and very little disturbance by the re-planting of new trees. In later years the wood was the favoured material for producing longbows, resulting in an act passed by Henry V to give the yew official protection.

# Alveley

Three listings of note for this name, as *Alvidelege* in 1086, *Aluitheleg* in 1195, and *Alfithelea* in 1196. Despite what was said about women's names being highly unusual in place names, this is the already the fourth example in the book and we are only halfway through the first letter. This name is derived from 'the woodland clearing of Aelfgyth'.

The pub here is the **Squirrel**, becoming increasingly popular as a name despite it having no true etymology. It seems to have been chosen simply because it allows sign painters to produce an image of this engaging creature which is instantly recognisable. Invariably it shows the red squirrel, still seen as this country's true inhabitant, even though few have seen anything but its North American cousin, the grey squirrel.

# Arleston

Recorded in 1180 as *Erdelveston* and thirty years later as *Erdulveston*, this is obviously a Saxon name from 'the farmstead of Eardwulf'.

Here we find the common name of **Chapel Yard** which refers to an early Methodist meeting place.

# Ashford Bowdler

Domesday's record of *Esseford* and the 1255 listing of *Asford Budlers* are all we need to define this name of Saxon origin. The elements *aesc* and *ford* tell us this was '(the place) at the river crossing by the ash trees'. To differentiate from the following place, the name of the early manorial family of de Boulers was added in the thirteenth century.

# Ashford Carbonel

Domesday's record is exactly the same as the previous listing as *Esseford* and is also from the Saxon *aesc* + *ford*, '(the place) at the ford where ash trees grow'. Again the addition refers to early lords of the manor, in this case the Carbunel family of at least the thirteenth century.

# Ash Magna

It may well be guessed that this comes from the Saxon *aesc* meaning '(place at) the ash trees'. Possibly there are those who could also see the Latin *magna* meaning 'great', to differentiate from the smaller Ash Parva.

The local here is **The White Lion**. Nearly always an heraldic reference, here it refers to the Earls of March.

# Asterley

Listed as *Estrelega* in 1208, this name comes from Old English *easterra* + *leah* giving 'the more easterly woodland clearing', suggesting it was probably an overspill settlement.

# Asterton

Only one early record of note, that of *Esthampton* in 1255. However, this can easily be seen to come from the Saxon *east* + *ham* + *tun*, giving 'the eastern home farm'.

# Astley

A fairly common name, always from the Saxon *east* + *leah* 'the eastern woodland clearing'. The only listing of note is as *Estleia* in Domesday.

Minor place names in this region include **Braidway**, an interesting evolutionary divergence from the usual Bradway or Broadway, which is what the name means. **Overmoor** speaks of 'the higher marsh', **Wheatley** is 'the clearing of wheat', and **The Dunstalls** speaks of where there were 'derelict buildings'.

For many years the dog has been the most popular pet in the country. Man's best friend was bound to appear on the signs of many pubs, sometimes as a breed but mostly as the faithful companion. The number of 'dog' names led to some inventive additions to make a place unique. One such pub is found at Astley; the **Dog in the Lane Inn**.

# Astley Abbots

As with the previous place the only early record is as *Estleia*, but dates from 1090. Not until the late thirteenth century do we find *Astleye Abbatis* to differentiate from the previous place. The addition refers to the early holding by Shrewsbury Abbey.

# Aston on Clun

Unlike other Astons in England, this place comes from *aesc* + *tun* 'ash tree farmstead', as evidenced by the 1291 listing of *Assheston*. The addition comes from the river name which, as discussed under its own entry, is of uncertain origin.

The local here is the **Kangaroo**, said to have been named owing to an early owner having Australian roots. Not only does the animal have a link to the country on the far side of the world, it is also an instantly recognised form, important when the hope is to attract custom.

# Atcham

With the only early listings available being Domesday's *Atingeham* and as *Ettingham* in 1199, it is difficult to tie the origins down with any certainty. It is probably a personal name followed by the Saxon *inga* and *ham*; in which case the origins are either 'the place of the followers of people of Aetti', or the personal name may be Eata (see below). However, the area could suggest the last element is Saxon *hamm* which refers to 'land in a river bend'. If this is the case then, once again, either personal name could precede it.

The church is dedicated to St Eata, the only one in England shown to be known as such. This seventh-century Bishop of Lindisfarne and Hexham in Northumberland does not seem to have any connection with Atcham whatsoever, although the possible personal name may suggest otherwise. However a photograph of crop markings here shows an outline of a substantial Saxon building, a pattern identical to a palace excavated at Hexham. It may be that a member of a prominent family came south from Hexham and brought the design along with the person's name. If this is also the basis for the name of Atcham, it is one of the few cases of the individual in a place name being identified.

The early forms are somewhat different to the modern spelling; however, this is undoubtedly down to local pronunciation. Interestingly, in 1785 Lord Berwick commissioned George Stewart to build the house and Humphry Repton to landscape the grounds of what is today the estate known as **Attingham Park**. The similarity between this name and the early forms of Atcham cannot be ignored. The answer lies beneath the Grade I listed building in the form of an earlier building designed and built by Richard Hill of Hawkstone. The landed gentry would have been able to read and will have based their pronunciation on what they read. The locals will have slurred the pronunciation and produced the modern name of Atcham; thus both forms are correct and have identical origins.

Alliteration is a powerful marketing tool which was seen many years ago. Pub names also seem to sound better from having two otherwise unrelated items joined. Furthermore the locals of a small community like their local to reflect that community. All three factors are satisfied by the **Mytton & Mermaid**, while producing a delicious sign to tell the story behind the name.

The man in question was Sir John Mytton, the local squire who died in 1834. His interest in the maids of Atcham is almost legendary; indeed the name is a play on 'mere maids', all that Sir John was interested in. He is shown on one side of the sign holding a foaming tankard of ale, with the mermaid emerging from the brew. Turn the sign around and see the story from the maid's point of view, where the mermaid is combing out her long hair and staring at the mirror where we see the image of Mytton wearing the most lecherous of grins.

*The gates of Attingham Park at Atcham.*

*The pub sign of the Mytton & Mermaid at Atcham.*

# B

## Badger

With listings such as *Beghesovre* in 1086, *Begesour* from about 1154, *Bageshour* in 1212, and *Beggesor* in 1229, we can be certain this name has nothing to do with Britain's largest carnivore. The suffix is Old English *ofer* which, when preceded by a personal name, gives us 'the hill-spur of a man called Baecg'. The modern form is simply a scribe's impression of the slurred pronunciation.

For those who may still hold that this was 'badger country', it should be noted that the Saxons described the creature as a *brocc* from which we get the term 'brock' today, or *bagge* which can be discounted with these early forms.

One name which has clear, and quite unusual, origins is the field name of **Innage** found here. This comes from the Old English *ineche* and refers to 'newly cultivated land'. To clear land for agriculture is no easy task, thus there must have been a real need. If we look on the plus side it may indicate a growing community, less favourably this may show the current land was no longer practical for a variety of reasons.

## Bagley

There are but two early forms of this place name, as *Bageleia* in 1002 and *Baggeleg* in 1225. As discussed in the previous entry, Saxon *bagge* described a badger. Indeed the popular definition is 'the woodland clearing where badgers are seen', the suffix from *leah*.

However Bagley is a fairly common name, with more than one origin. The personal name Bacga has certainly influenced some Bagleys, while Old Scandinavian *bagge* referred to 'a wether or ram', and Middle Dutch *bagghe* was 'a small pig'.

Furthermore there is the obvious 'bag-shaped woodland clearing' which, although it fits the name quite delightfully, is not really practical. The term was always used to describe a place which, in modern terminology, would be said to be a cul-de-sac, i.e. only one way out, as in a bag. It is difficult to see how woodland could ever provide a permanent obstacle; the axe or even the more drastic measure of fire would quickly have solved the problem. Without further documented evidence, the badger seems the most likely origin.

# Barrow

A very common name found throughout England and is normally, as here, from Old English *beru* or '(the place at) the grove'.

Local names include **Arlescott** or 'Eadwulf's cottages' and **Shirlett**, from Old English *scir hlet*, which is 'the shire allotment or allocation (of land)'. Two field names here are of particular interest. Firstly a derivation which will be encountered a few times in the county, here seen as **Fingerpost Ford** and which stands alongside the angle of a road junction, the name referring to the signpost. Then a name which does refer to events in the field, for the name of **Turn Again** tells that this field was ploughed, a comment which can be readily seen to have been made by some very tired ploughman!

# Baschurch

The eleventh-century listing of *Basecherche* and *Bascherche* together with *Baschirche* in 1167 show this to be derived from 'Bass's church'. The personal name together with Old English *cirice*.

It is not hard to see the **Boreatton Arms** as referring to the park of that name. A local family began construction in the middle of the nineteenth century, the design of the mansion being based on the calendar with fifty-two doors and twelve chimney stacks, each with seven pots. The original developer, who went bankrupt, and the consortium of businessmen who completed the project, are marked by the family shields lining the entrance hall. When it was finished in 1857 it became the home of the Hunt family. Thirty years later Dr Sankey made it an asylum for the insane. By 1942 the government opened it as a correction centre for delinquent boys, and by 1970 it was a community home. It was empty from 1974 until recently when the estate was adapted as a sports centre, utilising the grounds

*The Millennium Stone at Baschurch.*

for everything from football, rugby and tennis to horse riding with the lakes for canoeing. The sizable house is the perfect place to house the children who come to make use of the facilities.

# Battlefield

The first written record of this place dates from as late as 1415, when the place is known as *Batelfeld*. Being so late it comes from the Old French *bataille* which literally refers to 'the field of battle'. On the orders of King Henry IV the founding of a college of secular canons here, to commemorate the Battle of Worcester of 1403, was the birth of the settlement.

**Albright Hussey** is a small manor north of Shrewsbury. Listed as *Abretone* 1086, *Adbricton* 1242, *Addbrihton Hese* 1301, and *Adbrygton Husee* 1309, this tells us of 'Eadbeorht's farmstead'. The addition comes from the manorial holding of 1242 by Walter Hosey.

**Huffley** is another Saxon name speaking of 'the woodland clearing by a spur of land', while **Waits Coppice** is 'the coppice belonging to the (manor) house'.

Nothing to do with the actor, **Chevy Chase** is a name with a far more interesting background. It alludes to the ballad telling the story of the large hunting party riding through the Cheviot Hills. Led by Percy, Earl of Northumberland, the hunt is strictly against the wishes of the Scottish Earl Douglas. Making out the English hunt could be seen as an invasion, Douglas masses against the 'invaders' and an horrendously bloody battle ensues. Little more than a hundred left the battle scene alive.

In truth, history and folklore have become blurred and there are at least three ballads referring to several battles from minor skirmishes to full-blooded confrontations. Whatever the exact route to the name, to have origins from a fourteenth-century ballad is fairly unique.

# Bayston

Domesday's *Begestan*, together with *Beyston* from 1255 and *Beystan* in 1280, show this suffix to be from Old English *stan* rather than *tun* as we would expect from the modern form. Furthermore, the personal name to precede it is most likely that of a woman, not unique but fairly unusual. This place was founded as 'the stone of a woman called Beage'. The stone would have symbolised something, such as a meeting place, or a religious site, or a boundary marker.

In the village of Pulley is **Moneybrook**, a name which does not tell us there is a need to start panning for gold in these waters. Indeed the name is thought to have come from a field which was alongside the stream, itself taking this name because it was given as a charitable gift or a legacy. Stories of the river being where money was left for payment of goods during times of plague and thus to be cleansed by the waters, are without any basis in fact. Clearly these stories have been created to fit the name, rather than vice versa.

Nearby is **Welbatch,** a name literally meaning 'wheel stream' and doubtless referring to a water-powered wheel, yet unlikely to have been a mill or this would have been reflected in the name or documented. Any suggestions of what this wheel could have powered would be pure speculation.

**Eric Lock Road** is named after the RAF's flight lieutenant who was born in the village. He shot down sixteen or seventeen Luftwaffe aircraft during the Battle of Britain in September 1940, the highest number achieved by anyone. Despite being killed himself just twelve months into his flying career, he totalled among the highest success rate of any British pilot of the entire war.

Bayston has a pub called the **Three Fishes**. Although there are few pubs named such the others are thought to be heraldic. Here the reference is not to any local family; therefore it must be a link to Shrewsbury's fish market.

As with most places, the name of **The Beeches** simply speaks of what could be seen alongside the establishment. Although not particularly unique it does make an attractive sign and a fairly simple one.

There are many references in pub names to compasses, such as the **Compasses Inn** here. Very few show the ancient directional aid; most show the two-pointed geometrical instrument. The latter points to an early connection with a tradesman, likely to be a joiner or a carpenter for, as the name is plural, these coats of arms respectively show two and three such items.

# Beckbury

Many place names have an element from a Saxon or Scandinavian personal name. Over time this element is more susceptible to corruption and thus it is sometimes difficult to give that name and be absolutely certain of it. For example it would be virtually impossible to decide between Mick, Micky, Mike, Mikey, Michael, Mitchell, Michelle or Michaela over 1,500 years later.

The name of Beckbury has only two early records, that of the unreliable Domesday (as discussed in the introduction) being *Becheberie* and as *Beckebir* in 1229. Neither of these are particularly helpful in pointing to the Saxon personal name, however the suffix is quite clearly Old English *burh*, giving 'the stronghold of a man called Becca, Beocca, or similar'.

One farm has a name which is more common than one would think, although **Snowdon Farm** is not transferred from its better known namesake. Indeed both are from Old English *snaw dun*, literally 'snow hill'. The only surprise is that the local farm has not become Snowden; here the tallest mountain in Wales probably has an influence in the spelling.

The **Seven Stars** features an element which shows an association with religion. This particular pub shows no pictorial image; however it is often portrayed as the image of the constellation commonly known as the Plough, the best known of all in the night sky. Yet it is more likely that the addition of 'Seven' was to make it unique and for alliteration, a powerful advertising tool.

# Bedstone

With early records such as *Betietetune* 1086 and *Bedeston* 1176, the true personal name is difficult to uncover (see Beckbury above). The two listings found are quite different, although of the two, Domesday's is notoriously unreliable.

However what both listings do show is that the modern suffix suggesting a 'stone' is a corruption, for the true origin is undoubtedly Saxon *tun*. Taking names with similar evolution as a guide, the most likely origin for this name is 'the farmstead of a man called Bedgeat'.

# Benthall

This small settlement near Broseley is first recorded in the twelfth century as *Benethala*. This is from Old English *beonet* + *halh*, literally '(place at) the nook of land where bent grass grows'. Now obviously grass does not grow bent, although we must assume it describes a natural phenomenon. Thus the grass must be bent as a result of the action of wind and rain, rather than being trodden down.

Locally we find **Hunger Dale**, a name which does not mean what it seems but comes from Old English *hangra* or 'wood on a slope'.

# Berrington

Domesday's *Beritune*, together with later records of *Biriton* and *Byrinton* from 1242 and 1236 respectively, show this to be derived from two Old English or Saxon words. Here *burh* and *tun* combine to tell us this was once 'the farmstead of the fortified place'. This would suggest the earlier fortification was inhabited, but since the place was known by this name, it was simply a farming community.

# Betton

There are two places so-named in the county: one near Binweston, the other near Market Drayton. Both are from Old English *bece + tun*, 'the farmstead by the beech trees'. Interesting to note that none of the early records are alike until the fourteenth century, when they both appear in the modern form. Near the Welsh border, listings are as *Baitune* and *Bectona*, while near the boundary with neighbouring Staffordshire it was *Betune*.

Here we find **Alkmere** or 'Aelfgyo's pond', which has been greatly influenced by the name of Alkmund Park but has quite different origins. There is also the field name of **Four Acres** which is not a literal dimension but just 'very small' when compared to **Eight Acres** which simply tells us it was 'more than twice the size of Four Acres'.

# Bicton

Once again, as with the previous entry, there are two places with the same name in Shropshire. One near Shrewsbury is listed as *Bichetone* in 1086 and *Bykedon* in 1248, the other near Clun as *Bikedon* in 1302. Both have identical origins in Old English *bica + dun* speaking of '(the place at) the hill with the pointed ridge'. There are some sources that suggest the first element is a personal name, Bica. However this does not seem to fit the available evidence. In either case the existence of two identical names in the same county is purely coincidental and they are in no way connected.

View a map of the area and you will discover the Middle English field name of **The Pike**, a reference to the weapon and meaning 'a pointed shape', while **Ella Field** is from Old English *helde* 'the gentle slope'. Another of Old English derivation is the name of **Calcott**. From *cald cot* it refers to 'the cold cottages'; not that the buildings themselves here were particularly cold. Thus the meaning is probably cold as in 'shunned', an indication that the inhabitants were undesirable – literally given the cold shoulder.

**Rossall** is a name from 'the nook of land where horses are grazed', the suffix being Old English *halh*. **Udlington House** takes its name from 'Udel's Hill' on which it stands. **Bylet** is a common name found to describe the same feature as is seen here, the 'island in the Severn'. **Potch Green** speaks of 'soft ground'; indeed the verb 'potch' was very specifically used to describe the trampled muddy holes left by the feet of cattle and other ungulates.

Pub names here reflect both the locality, in the region which gave its name to the **Onslow Hotel**, as well as an obvious brewing name in the form of the **Grapes Inn**. The latter is a common pub name for it not only shows a fruit associated with wine, but affords sign painters a simple subject which is easily recognised.

# Binweston

The earliest record of this name is as *Binneweston* in 1292. This is so close to the modern form it really offers little assistance. As is often the case it is the personal name which is the stumbling block; the other elements are Old English *west* and *tun*. Most often the name is quoted as coming from 'the western farmstead of a man called Bynna', which would suggest there was once another settlement east of here with the same man's name. So far, research has failed to trace a plausible candidate.

# Bishop's Castle

It is not only unusual but quite refreshing to find a place name which has not lost the apostrophe before the possessive 's'. It is often a sign that the settlement was founded in comparatively recent times, indeed the earliest forms are as *Castrum Episcopi* and *Bisshopescastel* in 1255 and 1282 respectively. These show two languages which also indicate a more recent origin, Latin *castrum* and Middle English *castel*, both obviously referring to the 'castle' which was built on the order of the Bishop of Hereford in about 1127.

Pubs and churches have been always been linked since the days they were the only two meeting places in the community. Think of a bell and the first association is with a church and pubs were quick to utilise this simple symbol as a name. Obviously there would soon have been many named 'Bell' and differences were sought. One of the earliest was a number placed in front to indicate the number of bells in the church tower. At Bishop's Castle the **Six Bells Inn** is not only a pub but also a micro-brewery, enabling it to serve its own ale.

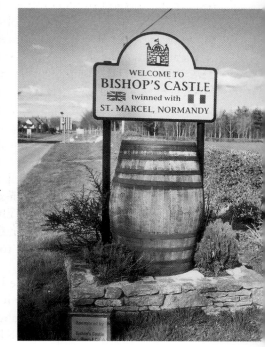

When the name refers to the pub itself it is common to find the wares advertised. Such is seen at the **Three Tuns Inn**, the tun being a large barrel for ale, and less obviously that of **The Boars Head**, which may seem to be heraldic but is actually a traditional Christmas centrepiece where the head is displayed with an apple or a lemon in its mouth.

*Bishop's Castle's continental town sign.*

# Bitterley

*The road sign at Bitterley with Titterstone Clee Hill in the background.*

Domesday's listing is, for once, closer to the true origin than that of today. Since 1086 as *Buterlie* and as *Buterle* in 1242, the name has changed in such a way that it now conveys almost the exact opposite message to the original Old English *butere* + *leah* 'the pasture that produces good butter'. The modern corruption is unfortunate, for surely the place would have been a marketing man's dream had it retained the original pronunciation.

# Bletchley

Records of this name are comparatively recent. *Blecheslee*, *Bleccheleg* and *Blecheleg* from 1222, 1254 and 1255 respectively, point to this originally being 'the place at Blecci's woodland clearing', the suffix coming from the commonly found Old English or Saxon *leah*.

**The Castle** is a local establishment with a name purporting to refer to the land historically being held by the occupant of the local castle or fortified manor house. While this may be the case on paper there seems to be far too long between the association and the naming of the premises and, despite the temptation, it is likely this was simply a case of the name being adopted as it is so easy to illustrate.

# Boningale

Our only early records of this place both date from 1285, as *Bolynghale* and *Bolinghale*. Although we cannot be certain of the personal name, the evolution in pronunciation from 'Bol' to 'Bon' is to be expected. With Saxon elements *inga* and *halh*, this is most likely 'the nook of land associated with Bola'.

# Boraston

An odd name with an unusual evolution, assuming the accepted definition is correct. The earliest records of *Bureston* and *Buraston*, from 1188 and 1256 respectively, are a little late to make definition easy. However it seems these are just slurred versions of the original Saxon *burh-east-tun* 'the fortification of or near the eastern farmstead'.

# Bouldon

Recorded as *Bolledone* 1086, *Bullardone* 1199, *Bolledon* 1199, *Bullardune* 1205, and *Bollardedon* 1242, these forms have left the first element uncertain. The suffix is certainly Saxon *dun*, 'a hill'.

The name has intrigued a number of individuals, for it is unusual to find so many forms recorded and still have few clues as to the origins. This has led to speculation that the name may not have originated here but was transferred when the settlement relocated by this hill. Consequently it is suggested that the first element is a corruption of *bula* 'bullocks', or the personal name Bula or Bulla. Unless we find earlier forms, some evidence of relocation, or a record of the supposed former settlement, these ideas will remain pure conjecture.

Inns have been named for a number of reasons; however, the **Tally Ho** is unusual despite being fairly common. It is associated with the cry sent out when fox hunting, drawing attention to their quarry in flight. However, while the link between the controversial sport and pubs is unquestioned, not every pub associated with the hunt can have been a meeting place for such. Thus the name is probably borrowed from the hunting phrase to suggest that everyone should be off to the local.

# Bratton

This name is found across the breadth of southern England as well as Shropshire. However this has a different meaning from the others, which all have a first element derived from Old English *braec*, 'newly cultivated land' (literally 'broken earth').

That found in Shropshire is also Saxon, this time the origins are *broc* and *tun*, as evidenced by the late eleventh century listing of *Brochetone* and giving 'the farmstead on or near a brook'.

At Bratton is a pub called **The Gate**. It is a simple sign and one easy to illustrate, indeed it is not unknown for a gate to be hung outside such-named pubs to act as the sign itself. To understand the name we need to examine the etymology of the word 'gate'. It comes from the Old English *geate* which does not have the same meaning historically. Today's gate is a doorway, referring to the door itself, while it was originally the way in, the actual road or pathway which allows access. Looking at Bratton's location it is easy to see how there are a number of potential access routes which could have given the name of the Gate.

# Bridgnorth

The first record of this name dates from 1156 as simply *Brug* which is from the Old English *brycg* and needs no explanation. By 1282 the place is known as *Brugg Norht*, the '(place at) the northern bridge', to distinguish from the Quatbridge which was lost soon afterwards.

Bridgnorth once had five town gates; remnants of Cow Gate can still be seen in the wall opposite Waterloo Terrace. The road leading down the slope here was **Cartway** which, before the new building was constructed in 1786, was the only way for carts to ascend from the wharfs along the river to **High Town**, named for obvious reasons. Stagecoaches would also use this road, pulled up the steep slope by the addition of extra horses stabled in the inns along here. When the carts were struggling up and down this narrow street their loads would threaten the glass in the windows of the buildings on either side, hence the shutters to protect them which are still visible today.

Continue down and arrive at where a series of dwellings were cut from the sandstone. Families would live in these cramped conditions and did so until 1856. With a total living area of just 10 square feet, they must have found life very difficult. It is rumoured the original iron cooking ranges are still in situ – if so they would be valued highly by the right buyer. Many of the houses down the street served as both alehouses and brothels, depending upon the demand. At its peak there were twenty inns along this small street, most of which were considered unsafe for they were the haunt of the Severn Sailors, a rowdy and boisterous crowd of dubious reputation. During the nineteenth century the standards rose so that Cartway housed carpet workers, barge workers and Irish farm labourers. The timber-framed house at the bottom of the hill was built in 1580 by Richard Forester, a wealthy barge master. Today it is known as Bishop Percy's House.

Modern licensed premises in Bridgnorth exhibit names from many different areas. Obviously the major attraction is drink, and pub signs were the perfect medium to advertise, the names were created as a virtual advertising slogan. The **Punch Bowl Inn** tells us that such would have been available within and what it was served in. We even know the origin of the name of this cocktail of drinks, not always necessarily alcoholic; it is derived from the word for 'five' on the Indian subcontinent. However, there has never been a suggestion that it should contain five different ingredients, or any other specific number. Similarly there can be no doubt what **The Cider House** hopes to serve to its customers.

It may seem that **The Ship** has obvious origins, although this far from the sea it is more likely to refer to an owner or landlord who had maritime connections. Similarly the **Cape of Good Hope**, another simple sign, would also indicate a former sea-going landlord. This kind of symbolism is the strongest theme for pub names, be it such obvious references or more subtle heraldic links. There can be no doubting the Irish implications in the name of the **Harp Pub**, with an easily recognised sign. However, the **White Lion** is less obvious and is a much more local reference to the Earls of March. Similarly the **Black Horse** may well be symbolic, such as seen in the modern Lloyds Bank logo. However, it was also a decent visual sign, suggested a blacksmith, a goldsmith in London, and is the nickname of the 7th Dragoon Guards. Just which of these and many other reasons it was chosen is rarely understood.

An unusual name is that of the **Lion O'Morfe**. References to lions are common in pub names, thus additions are sought for distinction. Here the close proximity to Wales has provided the word meaning 'marsh'. It hardly seems worthwhile mentioning there would have been half a dozen quite obvious trees alongside the **Six Ashes Inn**. The **Duck Inn** again is a simple sign and is normally found close to water.

While most signs will depict the **Black Boy** as the chimney sweep such as was seen in Kingsley's *The Water Babies*, the first reference was to the young flamboyantly dressed personal servants of the wealthy, the name also being popular for coffee houses.

To give a sense of personal service, landlords often gave their establishments names designed to attract local workers in a particular area. With the navigable Severn flowing through the town and the later coming of the railways we found the **River and Rail Country Inn** and the **Railwaymans Arms**.

Specific people and families were commemorated too, one of the most popular being the Bard himself, here being the **Shakespeare Inn**. The **Fosters Arms** was known as the Whitmore Arms from when it was opened in 1790. This honoured the family who had owned the estate for 250 years until it was taken over by the family after whom the pub was renamed, the family of one W.O. Foster.

There was a time when it was common for two signs to be amalgamated. This would happen when two individuals would unite in a new venture, bringing with them elements of their past lives – perhaps even the names of former pubs. Such happened particularly when very common names were involved, an example of which is the **Bell and Talbot**. The bell is common because it refers to the church and is an easily recognised shape. The Talbot is a breed of dog; white with black spots it was popular for its skills in hunting and tracking.

# Brockton

There are no less than three places of this name in Shropshire, all of which have the same origin. There is one near Lilleshall, another near Madeley, with a third close to Worthern, first listed over two centuries as *Brochetone*, *Broctone* and *Brockton* respectively. Coming from Old English *broc tun* this is easily seen as 'the farmstead by a brook'.

The local here is the **Cock Inn**, a name which is invariably linked with cock-fighting. It is true that pubs were often the venue for this so-called 'sport', yet for many years after it was banned it continued in secret. Clearly, to continue to advertise it as a possible venue by way of the name and sign was hardly the best method of keeping it secret. Hence most of these places are probably heraldic in origin, although there was a strange concoction popular in the seventeenth century called cock-ale which consisted of the jelly produced by boiling a cockerel which was mixed with ale and flavouring ingredients.

## Bromfield

*Brunfelde* in 1086, *Brumfeld* in 1155 and *Bromfeld* in 1228 are all little more than confirmation of the origins of this place name, which has evolved very little from the Old English *brom* and *feld* and describes the '(place at) the open land where broom grows'.

## Broseley

Despite three quite early listings of this name, we are unable to be certain as to the origins. As usual the problem is whether the first element is a personal name or not.

Records from 1177 as *Burewardeslega,* 1194 as *Burgardeslega,* and 1242 as *Borewardesleg* are still insufficient to determine if this is Old English *burh-weard* + *leah* giving 'the woodland clearing associated with the keeper of the fort', or 'Burgweard's woodland clearing'.

Around the town are found the **Instone** block of buildings, named after a local family. **The Burnt House** in King Street was partially destroyed by fire in June 1883. Indeed the name of the town is synonymous with that of a pipe tobacco, as evidenced by the Pipe Museum. Locally known as **Fiery Fields** where once flames leapt from a shallow coal seam and mining waste which were accidentally ignited.

*An unusual but attractive town sign.*

**Blakeway Close** takes its name from a draper in Shrewsbury and an influential figure at the Coalport China works, Edward Blakeway.

This parish has local names such as **Amies** from early ownership by William Amyas of Borewarsleye in 1327. Another local gave his name to **Jackfield**; once pastureland near the Severn belonging to John Jackes, it was later the site of a settlement dealing in the shipment of coal and iron.

**Ferry Road** comes from the ferry which ran from Jackfield to Coalport; it was made obsolete when the bridge was constructed. The Legg family made clay pipes; they gave their name to **Leggs Hill** where they lived and worked. **Prestage Close** is named after the tileries of that name, the remains of which can be found beneath the new estate. John Onions had a foundry on the site of **Foundry Road**. **Guest Close** is named after ironmaster John Guest.

**Fox Lane** was named after a pub, the Fox Inn, and **Cumberland Close** recalls the Duke of Cumberland, a public house on the corner of **Duke Street**, while Lord Forester of nearby Willey is remembered in **Forester Road**. **Woodhouse Road** is a tidied-up modern name, which sounds much better than the earlier Workhouse Road after which it was named until its demolition. A common street name is **Pound Lane**, always leading to or alongside the local pound where stray animals were kept until collected by their owners as soon as they had paid the fine.

**Astleyfields Colliery** took its name from the Saxon name of *aesc leah* or 'ash wood clearing'. **Rowton** and **Swinbatch** are also from the same Old English or Saxon language, speaking of 'the settlement at the rough place' and 'valley where swine are kept' respectively. Similarly the names of **Dunge Farm**, **The Dunge**, **Dunge Colliery**, and **The Dungegrove** all have their base in *dyncge* or 'the manured land'.

**Tarbatch Dingle** was known by the Saxons as *tar baece* and speaks of the bituminous wells which were worked here. Also from the same tongue and meaning 'silted land', here the basis being *wearp*, a place is now seen on present-day maps as **The Werps**.

The local here is the **Duke of York**, a popular name which may refer to any of the holders of this title since its creation in 1385 for the second son of the reigning monarch. Most signs depict the nursery rhyme of the *Grand Old Duke of York*, a song about Frederick Augustus, son of George III, who fought the French in Flanders at the end of the eighteenth century. It is an odd lyric for there are no hills at the battle site. At the time he was only thirty-one, and had thirty thousand men under his command.

# Broughton

There are a number of Broughtons in England, all of which come from Old English *burh* + *tun*, 'the fortified farmstead' or sometimes understood as 'the farmstead near the fortification'.

Here we find some unusual field names, such as **High Ferbirs Tenement** which is a rather lengthy way of describing 'the tiny enclosure with a house'. **The Wet Reans** is a field which had 'drainage furrows', while there has been an unusual corruption of 'dove house' leading to the modern **Duffers Yard**.

# Bryn

This name is easy to define for anyone who speaks Welsh, for it is simply the word for 'a hill'. Whether the name comes from the Welsh *bryn* or Celtic *brinn,* the meaning is exactly the same, although it seems certain the county's close proximity to Wales has affected the spelling.

Interestingly the earliest record of this place dates from 1272 as *Bren*. Thus we must assume the place took its name from the hill which had been known as such locally for several centuries.

# Bucknell

A name which was listed in Domesday as *Buchehalle*, in 1175 as *Bukehill*, and as *Bukenhull* in 1270. These do not adequately clarify the first element, so we are unable to tell if this is from Old English *bucca* + *hyll* 'the hill where male goats graze', or if the first element is the personal name Bucca.

Here are two pubs; the **Sitwell Arms** recalls the family who were influential in the area, while the **Baron of Beef** is a dish which would have been served here. The 'baron' is two sirloins still attached to the backbone, the name was created to suggest that the rank of baron was worth double that of a 'sir'.

# Buildwas

Early records of this name fail to point to an origin with any certainty. Recorded as *Beldewes* 1086, *Billewas* 1158, *Buildewas* 1169, and *Byldewas* 1248, the second element is clearly Old English *waesse* meaning 'alluvial land' i.e. land fertilised by seasonal flooding. It has been suggested that the first element is either *bylaw* 'builder' or *gabled* 'building', yet this does not seem to fit with the suffix and must be discounted. Without further clues the origins of the name will probably remain unknown.

# Burford

*Bureford* in Domesday is our only clue as to the origins. Basing a definition on the evidence of one record is not particularly easy. However, without further examples we can only assume this is Old English *burh + ford* as it seems, in which case the meaning is 'the fortified place by the river crossing'.

One of the most popular of all pub names, the **Rose and Crown** dates from the early seventeenth century and was designed to show loyalty to the country and its reigning monarch. Patriotism is still a powerful selling point, simply note the huge number of flags adorning pubs, particularly on the occasion of a major sporting event.

# Burlton

The earliest records come from the thirteenth century as *Burghelton* and *Burweltun*. These point us to the Old English *burh + hyll + tun* or 'the farmstead by the fort on the hill'. It is logical to assume that the original settlement was in the fortification on the hill. However, without evidence to show this, we must not assume that there was a migration from one to the other or that one of these places was permanently occupied.

Somewhat surprisingly for a small village, the local inn has been named after the place, residents enjoying a glass in the **Burlton Inn**.

# Burwarton

Domesday lists this place as *Burertone*, while by 1194 it had become *Burwardton*, only to appear in the modern form as early as five years later. This name has the same confusion as seen with Broseley, the first element may be the personal name Burgweard, or we could be looking at an origin of 'farmstead of the keeper of the fort' from Old English *burh-wear + tun*.

The **Boyne Arms** is one of the many pubs named after famous battles in history. The Battle of the Boyne was fought on Irish soil in 1690. It is seen as a pivotal moment in the relations between England and Ireland, the Catholics and Protestants, and the direction of the English Crown. It is likely a descendant of someone connected with the engagement was an early proprietor, although it may have been named by a supporter, an Irish Protestant who had come to Burwarton.

# C

## Calverhall

Whether we look to Domesday's record of *Cavrahalle* or the thirteenth-century listing as *Caluerhale*, this name is clearly of Saxon origin. From Old English *calfra* + *halh* it tells us this was the '(place at) the nook of land where calves graze'.

In effect, defining the name tells us something of the region during the late Saxon era, no matter how much the place has changed since. If calves are grazed here it tells us the quality of the pasture must have been reasonably good. Furthermore the term is specifically 'calves' which points to a permanent breeding herd. Sometimes defining a name can reveal rather more than one would imagine.

The **Old Jack Inn** here tells a general history of inns, yet also refers specifically to this establishment. Once there was a beer jug made from leather, coated on the outside with tar to seal it; it became known as a black-jack and was found throughout the land. Here there was an old vessel lined with horn and mounted on silver. It was brought out solely for village celebrations when, much like the famed yard of ale, many tried to drain it dry in one. It was the pub's most treasured possession until it disappeared in 1860.

## Cantlop

A rather unusual name which was recorded in Domesday as *Cantelop*. While the second element is clearly Old English *hop* 'valley', the first element has proved a stumbling block. The most likely source is the **Cound Brook** which runs through the valley. However the meaning of this name has proven even more difficult. The general opinion is that this is an early British or Celtic river name, which has the same beginnings as river names like Kennet or Kent.

*The ford at Cantlop.*

# Cardeston

Despite three records of this name being found, as *Cartistune* in 1086, *Cardistone* in 1275, and *Cardestone* in 1277, there is still some uncertainty as to the personal name. There is no doubt the suffix is Old English *tun* and the origin is something akin to 'the farmstead associated with Card'.

# Cardington

There is another place with exactly the same name in Bedfordshire. However the early forms are noticeably different, showing two different personal names have evolved to the same modern form.

Listed in Domesday as *Cardintune*, this is an Old English personal name followed by *inga* and *tun*. Although the personal name cannot be assured, this place comes from something akin to 'the farmstead of the family or followers of Card'.

Within the parish we find such names as **Battlestones**, a minor name which was originally applied just to the rocks at the top of **Willstone Hill**, itself named after the small settlement of 'Wulfhere's farmstead'. The 'stones' are the rocks but the 'battle' is not what it may seem; as a field name it refers to organised combat in order to finally settle a dispute.

**Waterloo Farm** is a name originally applied to the farthest corner of the parish, a 'remote' name doubtless influenced by the famous nineteenth-century battle. **Poulk Pool** comes from *puca*, suggesting the locals considered this place to be the haunt of a ghost, goblin or the like. 'Ceatta's spring' is on the map today as **Chatwall**; **Comley** is from *cumb leah* or 'the clearing in the valley'; **Yell Bank** is from *helde* or 'the slope'; and **Netchley** from *ecels leah* or 'the woodland clearing added to the estate'. With elements from Middle English *enche* and Old English *mersc*, **Enchmarsh** takes its name from 'the marsh of the servants'.

**The Royal Oak** is the second most common pub name in the country. It comes from the famed Boscobel Oak at Shifnal, where Charles II and his aide Colonel Carless hid in order to escape Roundhead troops following their escape from the Battle of Worcester in 1651. At the Restoration of Charles II it was declared that 29 May, the king's birthday, should forever be known as Royal Oak Day.

# Catherton

This name has only one early listing, as *Carderton* in 1316, which has made defining the first element difficult. While there is no possessive 's' in the modern form, this is by no means unusual and it is likely that the unknown is a personal name.

Although the evolution of the names has produced two different forms, it is quite possible the name is identical to that of Cardeston and therefore 'Card's (or perhaps Carda's) farmstead'. Note that even if the personal names are identical, it would not refer to the same person. The two places are about as far apart as it is possible to be and still remain within Shropshire, and travel over such distances would not have been commonplace.

# Caynham

It may seem that a succession of names have an uncertain personal name as a first element, as indeed is the case with Caynham. The problem can be seen if we look at familiar names today – Matt is easy to see as being from Matthew, but Dick from Richard, and what about Peggy from Margaret?

Recorded as *Caiham* in Domesday and as *Cainham* in 1255, the most likely definition of this name is 'Caega's homestead', with the suffix from Old English *ham*.

# Chelmarsh

Three early forms point to the origins of Old English *cegel* + *mersc*, the records of *Celmeres* in 1086, *Ceylmerys* in 1252, and *Cheylmerse* in 1255. Here is the '(place at) the marsh marked out with posts or poles'.

So why define the outline of a marsh with poles? Actually it is the drier regions which have been outlined, in effect a marked path to the settlement. Obviously those who lived here would already be aware of which route to travel; hence we can deduce the path was for the benefit of strangers or infrequent visitors. Furthermore this suggests these visits were welcomed and almost certainly for the purposes of trade. Chelmarsh may once have been an important trading post, a centre for commerce in the area.

Who would have thought a name telling of a few posts in a bog could have conveyed so much information?

# Cherrington

The early records of this name fall into two distinct groups, one suggesting three elements, the other only two. Listings such as *Cerlintone* in 1086 and as *Cherington* in 1230 point to the Old English personal name + *inga* + *tun* and 'the farmstead of the people or followers of Ceorra'.

However that of *Chorrintona* in 1181 could well be Old English *cerring* + *tun* which would give 'the farmstead in a river bend'.

# Cheswardine

A number of listings of this name have been found – *Cisworde* (1086), *Cheseuurda* (1160), *Chesewurda* (1169), *Chessewurda* (1178), *Chesewurdin* (1179), and *Chesewurthin* (1212). These point to Old English or Saxon *cese* + *worthign* telling us this was 'the enclosure where cheese was produced'. It must also have been a place with good grazing for even goats need a reasonable quality of pasture if they are to consistently provide enough milk to make the place known for its cheese.

Any pub named the **Fox & Dogs** will instantly be thought of as a meeting point for the hunt. While many do take their name from this now-banned bloodsport, the name is as popular in non-hunting country. This suggests either the name was transferred, brought with a landlord along with his sign, or the association has long been more with a pub than with the hunt.

# Chetton

Listings of this place include *Catinton* 1086, *Chatinton* 1167, as *Chetintone* in 1210, and *Chettynton* in 1254. This shows the origin to be Old English 'farmstead of the people or followers of Ceatta', with the personal name suffixed by *inga* + *tun*. Without the early records we would not have known about the element *inga*, thus showing the importance of consulting as many early records as possible.

# Chetwynd

A name which is recorded in Domesday as *Catewinde* in Domesday, as *Chetewind* in 1242, and as *Chettewinde* in 1233. A Saxon personal name with Old English *wind*, this is 'the place at the winding ascent associated with a man called Ceatta'. The close proximity of this with the following entry of Chetwynd Aston probably means the two have some historical connection.

# Chetwynd Aston

As with the vast majority of Astons, which is among the most common names found in England, it comes from the Saxon *east* + *tun* 'the eastern farmstead'. Listed as *Estona* in 1155, and as *Greate Aston alias Chetwynde Aston* in 1619, the addition is from 'the winding ascent of a man called Ceatta', as with the previous entry.

    The **Wheatsheaf** is a name popular in pubs as it refers to the product and is fairly simple to reproduce. Indeed the early sign of a farmstead offering their home brew for passing travellers would simply have been a sheaf of wheat or barley tied to a stake, thus the 'ale stake' and the beginnings of the classic pub sign.

# Chipnall

If we only had the modern form we would probably consider the suffix to be Old English *halh* 'nook of land'. However, by consulting early forms we find records of *Ceppecanole* in 1086 and *Chippeknol* in 1260 we can see the true suffix is *cnoll*.

    The first element is less certain. It may be a personal name and speak of the '(place at) the knoll of a man called Cippa'. Yet there must be nobody (other than Cippa's family and the man himself) who does not prefer the alternative *cipp* + *cnoll* which gives 'the knoll of land where logs are obtained'.

From an etymological viewpoint neither name has greater claim, while records are highly unlikely to be found to add weight to either argument. Indeed the major clue as to the correct origin depends upon when the place was settled and when the place was first named. If the name did not exist before it was settled, then the personal name is correct. However, if the name was used before settlement, then the alternative would be the beginnings.

# Chirbury

The earliest listing of this name dates from 915 as *Cyricbyrig*, later found as *Cireberie* in 1086, and *Chiresbir* in 1226. This is another name of Old English origins, from *cirice* + *burh*, 'the church of or near the fortified place'.

On nearby Stapeley Hill, which rises to a height of over 1,000ft above sea level, is a Bronze Age stone circle. Sometimes known as **Mitchell's Fold** it is also referred to as **Medgel's Fold**. The difference seems to be in pronunciation, for the origin is almost certainly Old English *mycel* meaning 'big' and a reference to the size of the circle rather than the stones themselves. It measures 89ft across at its widest point, making the circle slightly elliptical, the stones ranging in height from 10in to just over 6ft.

Unlike other stone circles, most notably Stonehenge, these are local stones. This may be significant for this is one of only three known stone circles in Shropshire; the others are **Hoarstones** and **Whetstones**. The latter stood less than half a mile to the east, although most of the stones were blown up in the 1870s and those that remain have fallen. In the holes were found the remains of fires and some bones, both animal and human. Hoarstones is a name said to refer to 'rough' stones, maybe in comparison to the neighbouring sites.

Folklore tells how Mitchell's Fold was created by a giant. Here he kept a cow, a beast that provided an endless supply of milk to all. However one old woman was not satisfied with simply filling her pail and tried to fill a sieve too. This enraged the cow who broke loose and made her way to Warwickshire, only to be slain by Guy of Warwick. Meanwhile the woman, found to be a witch, was punished by being turned into stone and then surrounded by the ring of stones we see today to prevent her escaping.

The **River Camlad** forms part of the border between England and Wales before running on to join the Severn. Its origin is certainly Welsh, yet it is unclear which of two equally plausible words is the real basis for the name. The two words have almost identical meaning when describing the river and pronunciation is also quite similar. It may come from *cam* meaning 'crooked' or from *cwlm* a verb meaning 'to knot'; either describe the twisting path equally well.

# Church Stretton

An element also found in the previous name is found for this place name. Here Old English *straet* combines with *tun* to refer to 'the farmstead on the Roman road'. In fact Shropshire's three Strettons each have distinguishing additions. Church Stretton is clearly a reference to the *cirice*, to differentiate from All Stretton and Little Stretton.

With this parish we find **Battle Field**, traditionally the site of the last stand by the British leader Caratacus against the Romans in AD 51, although there is no evidence to support this claim. **Helmeth Hill** takes its name from 'the elm trees at the slope to the hollow', while **Cunnery** is named for its 'rabbit warrens'.

**Worlds End** may not be particularly accurate as it only marks the southern parish boundary, yet **Motts Road** does commemorate Dr Charles Mott, a noted nineteenth-century local man. The oldest road here is undoubtedly **The Port Way**, a prehistoric track along the summit of the Long Mynd and thought to be part of the drover's route to Shrewsbury – for that is what *port* signifies, a 'market place'.

There can be few names more obviously referring to a pub than the **Bottle and Glass**. Simple designs, easy to produce and instantly recognised, it seems sign painters have (thankfully) yet to be tempted to depict any other image associated with the phrase.

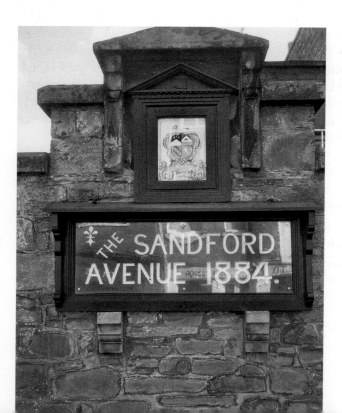

*Sandford Avenue, Church Stretton. Named after the Revd Mr Sandford who planted the trees along here.*

# Claverley

Domesday's *Claverlege* and *Clauerlai* in 1163 are records which point to the origin of Old English *claefre* + *leah*, or '(place at) the woodland clearing where clover abounds'.

# Clee Hill

While it may seem otherwise, this refers to the village and not the hill itself. As noted under the following entry, the hill name describes the shape of 'ball-shaped or rounded hill'. On the western slope is a road leading around an area of woodland, the conifers playing host to the red squirrel for as long as anyone could remember is today only marked by **Squirrel Lane**.

The **Golden Cross** seems to have no etymology associating it with the place, indeed no pub of this name can be explained fully. The cross, despite the temptation to suggest otherwise, does not normally have any religious connection but normally refers to a marker post, or maybe a crossroads. It seems the 'golden' addition was only to make it sound grander because of its humble beginnings.

The other pub in the village has a known etymology and a surprisingly recent one. The **Kremlin Inn** is the highest pub in the county of Shropshire, indeed it is said to be the highest point between here and a direct line to the Urals. This pub had always been known as the Craven Arms until the early 1970s. In those days licensing laws were different and pubs routinely closed at 2.30 p.m. until the evening session. To encourage patrons to leave promptly after the ten-minute 'drinking up' period, the juke box was normally switched off. However as the last '45 finished the (then) large box of equipment started to pick up and emit the sounds of Radio Moscow. Shortly afterwards the place changed its name, although there is still little to associate the place with the former Soviet Union.

# Clee St Margaret

Just two records of note here, as *Cleie* in Domesday and as *Clye Sancte Margarete* in 1285. The name of the hill, which is the basis for the place name, is thought to be Old English *cleo* meaning 'ball-shaped or rounded hill'. The addition is from the dedication of the local church to St Margaret.

## Cleeton St Mary

As with the previous entry, the basic name comes from that of the hill meaning 'ball-shaped or rounded hill'. Listed in 1241 as *Cleotun* the suffix is Old English *tun* giving 'the farmstead by the hills known as Clee'. The addition of St Mary, predictably, refers to the dedication of the church. However this addition is remarkably recent and has probably only appeared on most maps since the eighteenth century, although it is likely that the place was known locally as such well before this.

## Cleobury Mortimer

*Cleberie* in 1086, *Claiberi* 1201, *Claibur* in 1242, *Claibir* in 1266, and *Clebury Mortimer* in 1272 all point to yet another place name coming from the hill-name Clee. The suffix here is Old English *burh* giving us 'the fortified place by the hills known as Clee'.

The addition is a manorial one. One Ralph de Mortemer held this place at the time of the Domesday survey, yet the name was probably only coined when his namesake held the manor by 1236. The family name is itself from a place name,

Mortemer in France – which is situated on a hill and refers to an ox-bow lake created by the meandering Eaulne river, the name literally means 'dead pool' referring to the stagnant water.

One of the town's most famous residents in recent years is Simon Evans, a novelist, poet and broadcaster who came here after seeing action during the First World War to recover from the effects of poison gas used by the enemy. He took a job as a postman and walked 18 miles each day, growing to love the countryside and know the routes every bit as well as those who were born here. The air here clearly helped him extend his life considerably for it was not until August 1940 when he finally succumbed to the effects of the gas attacks almost twenty-five years earlier. The **Simon Evans Way** is a walking route named after him.

*The church at Cleobury Mortimer.*

Another pathway is **The Jack Mytton Way**, which takes a week to cover on horseback. Jack Mytton was a landowner, Member of Parliament, accomplished rider, enthusiastic fox-hunter, renowned gambler and Regency rake. Born in September 1796 he died short of reaching his thirty-eighth birthday having wasted the family wealth amassed over five centuries on a drunken spree and revelry which ended with him being remanded in the debtor's prison in Southwark, London.

Among his antics, he is reported to have hidden from his friends in the snow, swam rivers in full spate in the depths of winter, both times naked as he tossed aside every item of clothing when being 'caught up in the thrill of the hunt'. Some of his bets were unusual to say the least; none more so than in 1826 when he rode his horse into the Bedford Hotel in Leamington Spa (later HSBC bank). He rode up the grandest of staircases on to the balcony and from there, still in the saddle, leapt over the diners in the restaurant and out through the window back to the street below. These and many other reports of his antics mean he well deserved the epithet 'Mad'.

Less extrovert but equally deserving characters who have given their names to the streets of Cleobury Mortimer include **Grove Meadow**, named after Derrick Grove, a parish councillor who served for many years. However **Ralph Jones Terrace**

*Wells at Cleobury Mortimer.*

remembers a man who served a term of office which lasted just a few weeks short of fifty consecutive years on the parish council, while Ralph Jones was also governor of the Lacon Childe School.

**Hartmann Close** is named after Paul Hartmann, the Swiss-born director of the Müller food company, who also was among the founders of several local sports groups and societies. One man who worked for him at the company was Cyril Vaughan. Born in 1911 he was a postman before moving to Müller's, while also being known as a knowledgeable gardener and well-known character. He certainly merits the naming of **Vaughan Road**.

Pubs named the **Kings Arms** have been common since the Restoration of the Monarchy. Just which king the establishment is associated with is often difficult to see. This is not the case with the **Stables Tavern**, where the stables were virtually next door. The **Blount Arms** recalls the family whose lineage can be traced back to the Norman Conquest. The family tree is on display within the pub, while the sign displays the black and yellow shield which is their coat of arms. The French ancestry is the reason why the locals still pronounce the name as 'blunt'.

# Cleobury North

Records of this name date from the tenth century as *Ufere Cleobyrig*, Domesday as *Cleberie*, *Cleybiri* in 1241, and *Northclaibiry* in 1222. As with the previous entry the name of Cleobury refers to 'the fortified place by the hills known as Clee'. The addition is obviously to differentiate from Cleobury Mortimer, correctly telling us which settlement is the more northerly.

# Clive

The only record of any age is as the modern form in 1255. However there can be no doubt this is derived from the Old English *clif* meaning the '(place at) the cliff or bank'.

Locally we find **Drepewood**, a name from Old English *threap wudu*, literally 'the disputed wood'. Standing on the northernmost boundary of the parish it was doubtless the subject of hours of heated discussion. **Sansaw** is from the same Saxon tongue, where *sand–sceaga* describes 'a sandy coppice'.

While some field names can be seen as soon as the meaning is known, others require an expert eye. For example while names such as **Etches** 'the ash trees' and **Clemley Park** from *claeme leah* 'the muddy clearing' take only a few moments to recognise, we would not know 'brushwood' was the origin of both **Far Shrugs** and **Near Shrugs** were it not for the evidence of Middle English *scrogge*.

# Clun

Not only a place name but also a river name, the place being listed in Domesday as *Clune*. There is no doubt that the river held the name before the place, for the settlement is Saxon while the basic name is certainly British or Celtic. Unfortunately this name has never been explained with any degree of certainty.

*Clun Castle.*

*The River Clun.*

# Clunbury

Domesday lists this place as *Cluneberie* and there can be no doubt it means 'the fortified place on the River Clun'. The suffix is Old English *burh* but, as explained in the previous entry, the basic river name is unknown.

The local is the **Hundred House**, telling us it was where there was a regular meeting of those responsible for the hundred. The 'hundred' is a term used to describe the region into which the shire was divided since Saxon times. Despite reduction in the power of such courts, many of these continued into the latter half of the nineteenth century.

# Clungunford

Once again this name is based on that of the River Clun which, as noted under that entry, has never been adequately explained.

Listings of this place have been found from 1086 as *Clone* and from 1242 as *Cloune Goneford*. Although the basic name is unknown we can say this place is 'the place on the River Clone held by a man called Gunward'. Note the last two syllables are a personal name, the lord of the manor during the reign of Edward the Confessor. The modern suggestion of it being a 'ford' is a corruption.

# Clunton

Yet another settlement taking its name from the River Clun with its unknown meaning. Here the suffix is Old English *tun* telling us it is 'the farmstead on the River Clun', and was recorded as *Clutone* in 1086 and as *Cluntune* in the following century.

The local is the **Crown Inn Clunton**. The name itself is the biggest clue to the fact that it is a common pub name. The association with the monarchy is an obvious one, while the addition is to give it some degree of individuality.

# Coalbrookdale

This place was the birth of the Industrial Revolution. Mention this pivotal point in mankind's history and instantly we think of the steam engine and coal. It would be tempting to think this fossil fuel was the basis for the first part of the name or, failing that, we could find some influence by coal on this name. Sadly this is not the case. Coal as we think of it has virtually no representation in place names, any coal reference in names would always be to charcoal.

However the vast majority of 'coal' names are simply a corruption of 'cold', as is the case here. The earliest form found dates from 1250 as *Caldebrok*, which is from Old English *cald* + *brok* giving 'the valley of the cold brook' to which *dale* was added in later years.

# Cockshutt

Only one early record of note, that as *Le Cocksete* in 1270. This shows the name to be from Old English *cocc* + *scyte* 'a woodland glade where nets were stretched to catch woodcock'. Clearly two words would not convey such a complex or lengthy description. However, we know that woodcock was (and still is) considered a highly prized food item. It is not possible to physically hunt these birds, they are two small to warrant such an expenditure of energy despite being a ground-nesting bird. Furthermore when the female is on the nest their all-round vision, superb camouflage and lack of scent mean they cannot be located. Thus the method of trapping them in nets was the best method and it has been well-recorded.

To have this definition for a place name, the trapping of this bird must have continued for some time. Furthermore, there must have been a fairly good and reliable supply of birds, which would have made a valuable difference to the local economy.

However, to my mind it provides an instant image of the place, one which an artist could transfer on to canvas to show the lives of the people of Cockshutt in the thirteenth century.

Cockshutt is not the only descriptive place name here, for the local is the **Leaking Tap**. The general term brings forth an image somewhat different to that when it is associated with a pub. It seems unlikely that the name represents a place where there was a tap which leaked any more than any other tap. There are any number of reasons why the tap would be said to be leaking, however the most plausible explanation is the image showed the last drops of ale being poured into the tankard, said to represent a leaking tap.

# Colebatch

As with many personal name elements there is a degree of uncertainty to the origins of this place. The records start comparatively late, as *Colebech* in 1176. The suffix is undoubtedly Old English *bece* which, if this is a personal name, would give 'stream in a valley of a man called Cola'. However there is the alternative first element *col* meaning 'charcoal', i.e. where wood was smouldered by charcoal burners to produce charcoal for fuel.

# Colemere

A name recorded in Domesday as *Colesmere*, as *Culemere* in 1203, and in the modern form as early as 1274. This is an Old English name from *mere* and something very similar to 'the pool near the place of a man called Cula'.

# Condover

Records such as Domesday's *Conedoure*, *Cunedoura* in 1130, and *Cunedofre* in 1169 suggest this is another place name taken from the Cound Brook. However, as discussed under Cantlop, the name of this water course has not been adequately explained. Here the suffix is clearly Old English *ofer*, thus the best definition we can give is 'the place at the flat-topped ridge near Cound Brook'.

# Coreley

There is a very early record here of *Corna lip* in 917, which is followed late in the following century by *Cornelie* in Domesday. This name is from Old English *corn + leah* telling us it was 'the woodland clearing frequented by cranes or herons'.

The local here is the **Colliers Arms**, likely to have been for the benefit for those who were employed as such rather than being run by a former collier.

# Corfton

Only two records of note here, Domesday's *Cortune* and exactly as the modern form as early as 1222. This is an Old English name meaning 'the farmstead (or *tun*) by the River Corve'. The river name comes from the same ancient tongue where *corf* speaks of a 'pass'.

**The Sun Inn** is a common name for a pub. Aside from being a very simple sign to produce, and thus economical, it invariably depicts the dawn and implies a feeling of well-being with the return of the warmth of the new day, suggesting that a similar feeling can be found within.

# Corve

As stated under the previous entry the Old English *corf* tells of a 'valley or pass'.

# Cound

This place, listed in Domesday as *Cuneet*, stands on the Cound Brook. Quite clearly this has taken the name of the stream. However, the meaning of this early British or Celtic river name is unknown and seems destined to always remain so.

# Craven Arms

A name which, when compared to most, was created almost yesterday. The place was an important junction with the coming of the railways in the nineteenth century. It was this event which stimulated the expansion of a town that had been previously only the inn of that name built in about 1800.

The Craven Arms as a public house was named from the Earls of Craven who held land here. The name of Craven, a district in North Yorkshire, is thought to have come from an old Celtic name meaning 'place where wild garlic grows'. Ironically, while this is undoubtedly one of the most recent place names in the country, it has been transferred from a name which is one of the most ancient.

Of course this is not the only pub in the town. Another was built to mark the coming of the railways which created the expansion in the first place. Here, the name is fairly unique in the **Engine and Tender**.

*The public house which gave Craven Arms its name.*

# Cressage

For those who are reading this book from cover to cover at least, it cannot have gone unnoticed that the writer's personal favourite names are those which give a glimpse of a scene from Saxon times, a time once referred to as the Dark Ages, when recent research has revealed they were anything but.

The name of Cressage is somewhat different because it does not describe the place itself but a scene from village life. Recorded as *Cristesache* in 1086, *Cristesech* in 1185, and as *Cristeseche* in 1232, this is an Old English name from *Crist + aec* meaning 'Christ's oak tree'. This can only be a reference to a place where regular preaching took place. Furthermore, it shows that Christianity was alive and well in Saxon England during the depths of the so-called Dark Ages, not just providing a picture of the small community at worship but likely telling us which day of the week we are imagining.

With a name such as **The Eagles**, one local inn takes advantage of the majesty and power associated with this bird for millennia. Prior to this the sign is associated with Christianity; note the number of church lecterns decorated with the spreading wings used as a support. Inns and churches have had a close association since the time when they were the only two meeting places within a community.

# Crickheath

There are numerous examples of Scandinavian/Saxon hybrid names; however Celtic/Saxon connections are few and far between. Crickheath is one example, with elements from Celtic *crug* and Old English *haeth* 'the hill covered by heathland'.

Having defined this name we can deduce a little more information, even finding that the first element was the name of the place before any settlement grew here. How can we know that just from two words? Similar Celtic hybrids elsewhere prove the Saxons had no idea of the meaning of the earlier names – one example is Bredon, Celtic *brez* 'hill' with Saxon *dun* 'hill'. Thus the Saxon settlement was founded at a place they knew as 'Cruck hill', as evidenced by the 1272 listing as *Gruchet*.

# Crowmeole

Here the first element is exactly what it seems. This name is 'the place of crows on the Meole Brook'. Examined in greater depth under Meole Brace, this river name is likely to mean 'cloudy water'.

Locally we find names such as **Copthorne**, an Old English *copped thorn* or 'the pollarded thorn tree'. Pollarding was a system of managing young trees by cutting the top off at or above head height in order to encourage the growth of new wood in the form of poles which could then be used in construction. Cutting the tree at such a height prevented browsers eating the succulent new shoots as was the problem with coppicing. Another factor in the choice between coppicing and pollarding was the species of tree. Correct management of a tree can extend its life several times over.

Racecourse Lane marks the route taken to the racecourse at Shelton on a map of 1833, while The Russells is named after a family who were highly prominent in medieval Shrewsbury.

# Cruckmeole

In 1255 this place was recorded as simply *Mele*, however by 1292 it is found as *Crokemele*. The first element here is the same as is found in the following name, derived from Old English *croc* this is the '(place at) the river bend along the Meole Brook'. This ancient river name is thought to refer to cloudy water, as discussed under the entry for Meole Brace.

# Cruckton

From entries such as *Croctun* in 1272 and *Crokton* in 1308, this place is not exactly what we would expect it to be, i.e. 'the farmstead by the bend in the river'. Normally we would expect the first element to come from Celtic *crug*, however the forms are rather late for this. Furthermore, the topography of this region is better suited to Old English *croc* + *tun*.

The Hare and Hounds is a reference to the ancient bloodsport of hare coursing. It was banned in the UK in 2002 but is still practised elsewhere in the world.

# Crudgington

Unlike the previous entry of Cruckton the first element here is Celtic *crug* although the second element is not what the modern form would suggest. Listed as *Crugetone* and *Crugelton* in the eleventh and twelfth centuries respectively, the remainder of the name is Old English *hyll* + *tun*. This is therefore 'the farmstead of the hill called Cruc by the British'.

# Culmington

With early entries found as *Comintone* 1086, *Colmiton* 1160, *Colminton* 1161, and *Culminto* 1197, this is from a Saxon personal name followed by Old English *inga* + *tun*. This is therefore 'the farmstead of the family or followers of Cuthhelm'.

# D

## Darliston

The earliest listing so far found of this name comes from 1199 as *Derloueston*; fifty years later the name is found as *Derlawstun*. This is an Old English name from a personal name and *tun* meaning 'Deorlaf's farmstead'.

## Dawley

There is a place in Middlesex which has an identical name but a different origin, further evidence of the need to trace as many early forms as possible. Indeed the records as *Dalelie* 1086, *Dalilega* 1185, and *Daleleg* 1242 are quite different to those of its namesake. From an Old English personal name followed by *inga* + *leah* this was 'the (place at) the woodland clearing associated with Dealla'.

There are actually three Dawleys, all south of the main region which is now Telford. The additions for **Great Dawley**, **Little Dawley** and **Dawley Bank** require no explanation.

Locally in Great Dawley we find **Brandlee Lane** from 1780, **Brandley** from 1817, and **Branlea Hill** from 1833 together with several field names, all of which come from a single source of 'the burnt clearing'.

**Castle Pool** is a reference to a manor house, fortified in 1316 and now buried under a nineteenth-century slag heap.

**The Finger** is a field by a junction of five roads; recorded as *Peter's Finger* in 1833 it refers to the signpost which once stood here. From there came the name of **Finger Road**.

**Frame Lane** led to the former *Frame Wood*, itself telling us it was where timber was obtained for building.

**Church Road** leads to the church dedicated to St Leonard.

Little Dawley boasts **Croppings Farm** where there is 'an outcrop' of rock, **Lightmoor** is from *leoht* and *mor* 'light moor' and a reference to the vegetation, and **The Old Wind** refers to the incline with its natural up-draught. **Shop Lane**, despite what it might seem today, comes from *sceoppa* meaning 'shed'. Finally there is **Botany Bay Colliery**, which took its name from the field here. In later times it was often the norm to give the farthest point of the settlement a 'remoteness' name, and there was none more remote than the bay first seen by Captain Cook when he mapped Australia.

Pubs here include the **Station Inn**, created along with the railway and remaining after its demise. The reference to the monarchy is clear with the **Queens Arms**, yet the **Three Crowns Inn** is more likely to symbolise the Worshipful Company of Drapers, a former trade of the inn-keeper perhaps? As has been said elsewhere in this book, there has always been a close association of public houses and churches ever since they were the only meeting places in a community. Hence the name of the **Church Wickets**, although this has nothing to do with England's national summer sport but is a reference to a split door. A 'wicket' was only found in a large double door, a smaller point of entry built within the main door itself.

# Deuxhill

Listed as *Dehocsele* in 1086, *Deukeshull* in 1203, and *Dokeshull* in 1291, this name possibly refers to 'Deowuc's hill'. Indeed from a charter of 963 comes the name of a now-lost *Diowuces Path*. Here is the minor place name of **Horseford Bridge**, clearly the 'horse's ford alongside a footbridge'.

# Diddlebury

Records of this name include *Dodeleberia* in 1090, *Dudeneburia* 1147, *Dudeleberi* 1193, and *Dudelebur* 1242. Here the Saxon personal name is followed by *burh* giving 'the stronghold of Duddela'.

**The Sun Inn** has long been a favoured pub name. A combination of a simple sign, easily portrayed, and suggesting a warm and friendly atmosphere within has readily given itself to the name of a pub.

# Dinchope

Two twelfth-century records show there is actually another element in this name, one that has been lost over the centuries. Both *Dudingehope* and *Doddinghop* show this is from a Saxon personal name + *ing* + *hop*, giving us the '(place in) the narrow valley of the family or followers of Dudda'.

# Ditton Priors

The value of examining early records is seen in the previous entry of Dinchope. Once again this place shows the need to ensure the basic name of Ditton is, along with every other similar name in the land, from Old English *dic-tun*. In fact the listings of *Dodintone* 1086, *Dodointon* 1160, *Dudinton* 1212, and *Dudinton* 1230 show the Saxon origin to be 'farmstead of the family or followers of Dodda (perhaps Dudda)' with the personal name suffixed by *inga* + *tun*.

Although there are no other Dittons in Shropshire, the nearest being in Cheshire, there is an addition to differentiate. This is a manorial addition referring to Wenlock Priory.

Here we find the name of **Horseley's Coppice**. While the second half of this name is self-explanatory, the first word is among the most corrupted names in the county. This began life as *Eard's leah* (woodland clearing), which we would have normally expected to find as 'Ardsley'. The modern spelling is entirely down to incorrect pronunciation historically.

**Powkesmoor Farm** is from the Old English *puca mor helda* or 'the goblin marsh and slope', while **Bent Lane** owes its name to *beonet* as it is 'where bent grass is seen'. **Thirteen Butts** may seem a strange name, yet simply refers to the number of strips of land in this field. **Derrington** began life as 'Deorga's farmstead'; **Sidnall** is from *sid halh* or 'the wide nook of land'; **Ashfield** or *aesc feld* is 'the open land by the ash trees'; and **Great Hudwick** 'Hudda's Wick' the addition to distinguish with a similarly named smaller settlement which is no longer in existence.

# Doddington

Listed in 1285 as *Dodington*, this quite common place name is derived from a Saxon personal name with *inga* and *tun*. This gives us a definition of 'the farmstead of the family or followers of Dudda'.

*The view from Doddington across Shropshire.*

# Donnington

This is a quite common place name, indeed there are two in Shropshire alone; one is north-east of Telford and the other 9 miles south-west. That the two are fairly close together and neither has a defining second element is somewhat surprising.

Both are derived from a Saxon personal name with *ing* and *tun*, giving 'farmstead associated with a man called Dunn or Dunna'.

The local here is the **Champion Jockey**, a name which refers to the birthplace of Sir Gordon Richards at nearby Oakengates. During his long career, the first knight of the racetrack rode 4,870 winners and was champion jockey twenty-six times. In recent years his record for the most wins in a season has been exceeded by Tony McCoy, yet in the modern age when helicopters and planes can shuttle jockeys from one meeting to the next in the same day the present-day jockey has more opportunity to ride winners. Taking everything into account there has yet to be a rider who has ever come close to Sir Gordon's achievements, even though he retired in 1954 following an injury just a year after he finally managed to win the coveted Epsom Derby for the first time. The Oakengates Theatre has a Pinza Suite which was named after the horse which gave the famous jockey his one and only Derby victory.

# Dorrington

A name which is so similar to the previous two (in fact only one letter different) it is likely to be of similar derivation. Indeed the listing of *Dodington*, found in several documents from 1198, does show that this has very similar beginnings as 'farmstead associated with a man called Dodda'. The Old English personal name is suffixed by both *ing* and *tun*.

The **Bridge Inn**, which also runs a camping and caravan site, takes its name from the river crossing which has been here longer than any.

# Dudleston

No surprises with this name, although there is a little uncertainty as to the personal name. Recorded as *Dodeleston* in 1267, the Old English suffix is *tun* and tells us this was 'the farmstead of a man called Duddel or Doddel'.

# E

## Eardington

A name listed as early as 1030 as *Eardigtun* and as *Ardintone* in Domesday. Here is another Saxon personal name with Old English *inga* + *tun*, giving 'the farmstead of the family or followers of Earda'.

## Easthope

Domesday lists this place as simply *Stope*, with *Esthop* found in a record dating from 1242. However the earliest listing comes from 901 when, amazing as it may seem, the name appears exactly as in the modern form. Having examined literally hundreds of place names throughout England, never have I found an example of a name from a Saxon record some 1,100 years ago with the spelling exactly as it is today.

This is from Old English *east* + *hop* '(place at) the eastern enclosed valley'. It seems likely, as there is no mention of the settlement in the name at any stage over its evolution, that the name was given to the valley many years before the settlement began and took on the same name.

One local name is highly descriptive. With origins derived from Old English *cocc sciete* this is 'the muddy or dirty heap', today known as **Cockshoot**.

## Eastwood

Despite what the modern form of the name says, the origin is not quite as obvious as it would seem. With listings such as *Estewic* in 1086, *Estweit* in 1165, and *Est Twait* in 1166, this is a hybrid name with Old English *east* together with Old Scandinavian *thveit*. This points to '(place at) the eastern clearing', hence it is not the wood itself that is being referred to but 'a woodland clearing'.

Domesday's listing as *Estewic* would seem to suggest the suffix is Old English *wic* 'specialised farm' and usually a dairy farm. However the rest of the forms do not confirm this and, with the unreliability of Domesday as discussed in the introduction, this particular record can be discounted as erroneous.

# Eaton

One of the most common place names in the country, indeed there are at least three in Shropshire alone. However there are two different origins, as we shall see.

The vast majority come from Old English *ea* + *tun* 'the farmstead by a river', and there must have been many examples of such for a reliable and close water source must have been as important to Saxon farmers as it is to their twenty-first century counterparts. Both Eatons, one near Bishop's Castle the other near Ticklerton (see the following entry), are recorded in Domesday as *Eton*. That they are only approximately 8 miles apart makes it somewhat surprising that there is no second element to distinguish between them. This probably indicates there has never been a common landlord for both. However there is a second element for the following entry.

# Eaton under Heywood

This place near Ticklerton is sometimes given as simply Eaton. The addition comes from Old English *haege* or *hege* + *wudu* 'within or near the enclosed wood'.

Among the local names of interest, all of which are of Old English derivation, are **Harton** from *haer tun* 'the farmstead at the rock'; **Wolverton** or 'Wulfhere's farmstead'; **Whitbach**, 'the light-coloured place near the stream in a valley'; **Ticklerton** is 'Tyclea's enclosure'; **Birtley**, 'the woodland clearing near the little birch trees'; **Hatton**, 'the farmstead in heathland'; and **Hungerford**, 'barren land over the River Corve'.

The name of **Saplings** has nothing to do with trees, for there are none marked on any map since the name first appeared, hence the most likely origin is that this exhibits a possessive 's' and is a personal name. The unusual name of **The Velvetches** comes from *feld baece* and is 'the open land near the stream in a valley'.

# Eaton upon Tern

As with the previous entries of Eaton this name comes from Old English *ea* + *tun*, 'the farmstead by a river'. That this has a distinguishing addition, while the previous two do not, is surprising for this Eaton in Shropshire is some 30 miles distant from the others.

The addition, not surprisingly, is the name of the river upon which it stands. **Tern** is a Celtic name and, as with the vast majority of the early river-names, is highly simplistic. Here the meaning is literally 'the strong one', clearly a reference to the current.

# Edge

Only one real listing of note for this name, as *Egge* in 1255. However no matter when the listing dates from this can easily be seen as coming from Old English *ecg* meaning the '(place at) the edge or escarpment'. There is no doubt this place is aptly named.

# Edgmond

An Old English personal name followed by *dun* is the basis of the evolution of this name from Domesday's *Edmendune* 1086, through *Egmendon* 1165, to *Egmundon* in 1227. This is 'Ecgmund's place at the hill'.

The **Lamb Inn** was probably originally a link with the church, however today it is just as much associated with the shepherd.

# Edgton

From Domesday's *Egedune* to the thirteenth-century *Egedon*, all the forms point to a similar origin as the preceding name. Here the personal name is different but the suffix is still Old English *dun*. This place is 'Ecga's place at the hill'.

# Edstaston

Here is a name recorded as *Stanestune* in 1086, and as *Edestaneston* in 1256. Domesday's record must be regarded as erroneous, for reasons discussed in the introduction. The second element here is Old English *tun* preceded by a personal name and giving us a meaning of 'the farmstead of Eadstan'.

# Ellerdine Heath

A name of Old English origin, recorded as *Elleurdine* 1086, *Elleuwurth* 1196, and *Elleurwurthin* 1212. Here 'the enclosure of a man called Ella' has the personal name and the element *worthign*. It should not be seen to be a defensive enclosure, to deter warring tribes, but a stockade to protect livestock from predation.

The addition of 'Heath' is self-explanatory, yet what is interesting is just how recent the addition is. It seems to have only been an official name since Victorian times; however it is likely the name had been in use locally for some considerable time before this.

## Ellerton

The thirteenth-century listings of *Athelarton* and *Ethelarton* tell us this is an Old English place name, a personal name preceding *tun*. Here we have 'Aethelheard's farmstead'.

## Ellesmere

Despite Ellesmere Port being the better known, this is the original name. Indeed the Cheshire version took its name from the Ellesmere Canal which joins the Mersey at that point and is therefore only nineteenth-century.

The original Ellesmere is listed in Domesday some 800 years earlier. Records of *Ellesmeles* 1086, *Ellesmera* 1172, and *Ellesmere* 1200 are quite consistent and show this to be from 'Elli's lake or pool'. The elements are a Saxon personal name with Old English *mere*.

*Ellesmere's lake.*

The glacial depression formed the largest natural lake in England outside the Lake District. The island in the centre is man-made, formed from the spoil heap created when the gardens were dug for Ellesmere House in 1812. This date is relevant for it was the year Napoleon was forced to withdraw from Moscow, although it was a few years later that the island became known as **Moscow Island**.

In Ellesmere there is a **Market Hotel**, named for obvious reasons, while the **White Hart** may originally have been representative of Richard II but today it is often used as a generic term for a pub.

*The canal at Ellesmere, just before it enters the 80m-long Ellesmere Tunnel.*

# Ercall

There are two Ercalls in Shropshire, approximately 6 miles apart. The basic name is an unusual one and seems to be from a hill name *Earcaluw* from Old English *ear* 'gravel, mud' and *calu* 'bare hill', the two together describing land which would have been quite unsuitable for cultivation. However we have already said that these places are quite distant and there is certainly no hill of this size linking the two. So there must be some other reason for the name to be common to both sites. Normally the answer would be unknown and we would have to suppose it was transferred by some of the inhabitants relocating. However, here the name was (for a short time) used as the name of the district. Indeed, one could say the name was transferred via the map.

The two places each have an addition to distinguish them. **High Ercall** is listed as *Magna Ercalewe* in 1327, which is from the Latin meaning 'great', telling us this was the larger of the two in the fourteenth century. **Child's Ercall** appears in the same year as *Childes Ercalewe*, an Old English *cild* meaning 'son of a noble family' and a reference to the manorial holding.

Here the **Cleveland Arms** denotes land held by the dukedom created in 1670. Normally the many illegitimate offspring of the king were never recognised as such, despite quite frank acceptance that they existed. In rather unusual circumstances one Barbara Palmer, a mistress of Charles II, was given the title and special conditions were applied allowing the illegitimate result of their liaison, Charles FitzRoy, to inherit in 1709. The title passed to his son William and then became extinct until it was revived in the middle of the nineteenth century for his great-grandson.

## Eyton upon the Weald Moors

As English a place name as it is possible to find. The entry in Domesday is as *Etone*, so we shall examine this basic name first. The origin is Old English *eg + tun* meaning 'the farmstead on dry ground in marsh'. Meanwhile by 1344 we find this place as *Eyton super le Wildmore*. It is not difficult to see this addition as 'the wild moorland', the Old English origin being *wilde + mor*.

Local names include **Wappenshall** or '(place at) Hwaetmund's nook of land' and **Shawbirch** which comes from *sceaga* and *bryce* 'the newly cultivated land'. **Mantle Covert** is a name describing the shape of the place, said to resemble a cloak (if a cloak can be said to have a shape). While **Hogg's Pasture** may be seen to refer to pigs, early records show this is a dialect word *hag* meaning 'coppice', which comes from Old Norse *hogg* and describing 'the part of the wood put aside for cutting'. Lastly is the unlikely seeming name of **Commission Drain**, a name coined following the appointment of commissioners under the Wildmoor Inclosure and Drainage Act of 1801.

# F

## Farlow

The three records of note are from across several centuries, showing the evolution of the name quite well. Domesday's *Fernelau* from 1086, followed by *Ferlaue* in 1206, and *Ferlowe* in 1433 all point to the origin of Old English *fearn* + *hlaw*, giving us 'the hill covered with ferns'. It seems logical to assume this was a name given to this place before it was settled, for the name contains no trace of any mention of habitation.

## Felton

A name found in a few places around England, always with the same origins of Old English *feld* + *tun* 'the farmstead in open country'. There are two places with this name in Shropshire, which are both recorded as *Feltone* in Domesday, with later records of *Felton* in 1265, and *Felton Butiler* in 1230. The latter is today known as **Felton Butler**; the Buteler family were lords of this particular manor from the twelfth century. Some 5 miles distant lies **West Felton** which is a rather odd name for it lies almost directly north of its namesake. We can only assume it was in the western area of land held by a landlord and that the direction does not refer to its relative position to its namesake.

## Fitz

An unusual place name and one which has been somewhat corrupted since its early days as *Witesot* 1086 and *Fittesho* 1194. The only possible origin here, if we discount Domesday as erroneous, is a Saxon personal name with Old English *hoh* giving (place at) the hill-spur of a man called Fitt'.

# Ford

A common enough name, although only found alone for a main place three times in England. The vast majority of these names are minor place names, at the most names of districts and usually a much smaller area.

The Shropshire chapter of Domesday records the name as *Forde*, which is from Old English *ford* and is exactly what it seems, 'a river crossing', or more accurately the settlement on or near same.

Here is the **Cross Gates Hotel**, a name taken from an old area shown on maps as Cross Gates. In earlier times a Saxon *geate* referred to the path allowing access to or from a region, not the doorway itself; literally it was the way in and out. This point would have been where two or more such paths crossed.

# Forton

As with the previous name, a common place name although one normally found as a minor name. The origins of all are Old English *ford* + *tun* 'the farmstead by the ford'. Shropshire's Forton is recorded in 1086 as *Fordune* and in the modern form as early as 1240.

# Frankton

This name is derived from an Old English personal name with *tun* giving us 'Franca's farmstead'. There are actually two places with this name in the county, **English Frankton** and **Welsh Frankton**, the latter 5 miles further west and only closer to Wales, not in Wales. Just one record is found in Domesday, as *Franchetone*, while the first mention of *Elnglyshe Frankton* and *Welsch Francton* are from 1577. It seems certain that they were originally one settlement, one being an overspill of the other.

# Frodesley

Even Domesday's *Frodeslege* is similar; indeed both show the possessive 's' element following the personal name. Here, with Old English *leah*, the name can be seen as 'Frod's farmstead'.

# G

## Glazeley

A name recorded as *Gleslei* 1086, *Gleseleia* 1994, *Gleseleg* 1230, and *Gleseleye* 1270, none of which help us to define the name with any certainty. It is the first element which is proving elusive and, for once, it is unlikely to be a personal name.

One suggestion is that this is Old English *glaes* + *leah* or '(place at) the bright clearing'. If this is so it may be an indication that this was a former marker on a ley line, the ancient paths which enabled travellers to find their way through the almost complete woodland of England. Whenever possible water made a perfect marker, even on the dullest days the light is reflected from the surface of a pond or spring, making it stand out.

Another idea is related to Welsh *glais* meaning 'stream', although the supposedly lost Old English *glaes* as a stream name would need to be trusted without a single scrap of evidence. However if this is the derivation, it would be telling us of 'the woodland clearing of the bright one (i.e. the stream)'. Despite the lack of evidence, this is the most promising definition.

## Golding

Old records of *Goldene* in 1086 and as *Golden* in 1222 show this to be from Old English *gold* + *denu*. This name is derived from '(place at) the golden valley', probably a reference to soil colour. It has been suggested that the 'gold' referred to yellow flowers which grew here, even suggesting the origin as *golde* which referred specifically to marigolds. However the floral origin would have only been applicable during short periods of the year. Hence the most likely explanation is a sandy-coloured soil.

# Great Bolas

The first part of the name is an obvious reference to this being the larger of two settlements with identical names. This can be seen in the early listings as *Belewas* 1198, *Bowlewas* 1255, *Boulewas* 1265, *Bowelewas* 1293, and *Magna Boulwas* 1327, the final record with the Latin *magna* or 'great'.

Despite the number of records available, they are comparatively later than we would hope to assist in defining a place name. While the suffix is undoubtedly Old English *waesse* 'alluvial land, subject to seasonal flooding', the first element is uncertain. There are two possible explanations. The first is Saxon *bogel* 'meander, or gentle bend in a river' which would fit in with the general picture and is the most popular explanation because of this.

However the records may suggest that the modern name is a shortened version of the original Saxon *boge-leah-waesse*, the first two elements are literally 'bow woodland clearing', suggesting this was a place where trees were pollarded in order to produce long straight poles for use in bow-making.

# Great Hanwood

Domesday records this place as simply *Hanewde* which, along with the dearth of other forms, makes defining this name difficult. Indeed there are three equally plausible origins for the name of Hanwood, all of which are Old English.

Firstly we have *hana* + *wudu* which is '(place at) the wood frequented by the cocks of wild birds'. There is also the possible first element *han* meaning 'rock, stone', speaking of a prominent and probably quite large boulder nearby. Finally the third alternative is the personal name of Hana. The additional Great has obvious meaning.

The only name of note here is **Thieves Lane**, which should not be taken literally as it was more likely to have been used to describe the road taken to where undesirables were in residence.

# Greete

A name found in three counties with identical origins. Even without the records of *Grete* 1183 and *Groete* 1278 we could easily see this as Old English *greote*, 'a gravelly place'.

# Gretton

No shortage of early records for this place. From Domesday in 1086 to the record of 1327, we find *Grotintune*, *Grotintun*, *Grotington*, *Gretinton*, and *Greotytone*. Undoubtedly this Old English name is from *greoten* + *tun* or 'the farmstead on gravelly ground'.

# Grinshill

Early records here are inconclusive, the name remains uncertain. However this does not mean we can offer no possible origins, indeed we do know the name is certainly of Old English derivation.

This place may be from *grynel* + *hyll* which would be 'the snare for wild animals on a hill'. If this is the case the name (and therefore the trap) would have existed well before any settlement was built. However it may be that the pronunciation of the name in early times may have been slurred and become corrupted. The suggestion is that the name was originally *Gren-hyll*, 'the green hill', and that the modern second element is in fact a second 'hill' element. Without further evidence the origin will remain unclear.

**Sansaw Heath** is a name 'borrowed' from Sansaw in neighbouring Clive, where the name tells of 'the sandy coppice'. **Barn Horn** has nothing to do with farm buildings or animals; it describes 'the curved strip of cultivated land'. A lane in the south of the village is known as simply **Foredraught**, a name which reveals a picture of the place in early days when it was used as 'the road along which cattle were driven'.

# H

## Hadley

It is hardly surprising that this is a common place name, considering its origins. Listed in Domesday as *Hatlege*, in 1191 as *Hadlega*, and in 1238 as *Hathlegh* this name comes from Old English *haeth + leah* or 'the woodland clearing where heather grows'. It should be noted that although the name is commonplace, it is also found in the twenty-first century as Hadleigh.

Minor names in Hadley are varied, although several owe their existence to the Shropshire Union Canal. **Turnip Lock** was constructed next to a field where this crop was being grown at the time. **Shucks Lock** tells us it was a muddy place before the canal arrived. **Peaty Lock** has a name which speaks for itself, and has identical origins to the completely different name of **Mump Moor** which is where peat was dug. **The Harbour** is a common field name which is a corrupted version of *eorth burh* 'the earth fort', **Leegomery** is Saxon *leah* with the family name de Cumbray, and **Apley** from *aeppel leah* or 'the apple woodland clearing' – although this would refer to the gathering or storage of the apples.

The often-found link between church and public house is seen at Hadley, albeit a more subtle reference. Pubs named the **Cross Keys Inn** always refer to St Peter, the papal coat of arms also depicting this image.

## Hadnall

Records of this name are found as *Hadehelle* 1086, *Hedenhola* 1167, and *Hadenhale* 1242. This is an Old English or Saxon place name with the suffix *halh* telling us it was originally '(place at) Headda's nook of land'.

Within the boundaries of Hadnall are a number of names of interest. **Hardwick Grange** is a grange of Haughmound Abbey and has a name which comes from Old English *heorde – wic*. As discussed elsewhere in this book, the Saxon *wic* refers to a 'specialised farm' which in the vast majority of cases refers to a dairy farm, although we can never be sure unless there is further evidence. In this case that evidence is here in the shape of the first element *heorde* or 'herd'.

From Old English *haga - stan*, meaning 'the stony hedged enclosure', comes the name of **Haston**.

**Painsbrook** is named after William Payn, who owned a house and land here by 1240. The place known to be 'the cottage of the smiths (metalworkers)' is today found as **Smethcote**. From the *bryce*, literally 'speckled' and referring to land where vegetation was patchy, comes **Wheat Breach** which in turn gave rise to **Wheat Croft** and **Wheat Field**.

**Rabbit Hill** needs no explanation; however it was probably changed deliberately for the earlier names were *Gorsty Bank* 'the gorse-covered slope' and earlier *Gallows Tree Bank* where the name was not only obvious but ominous.

**Merry Lane** comes from the Old English *maere* meaning 'boundary'. In fact it does stand on the border between here and neighbouring Clive, where there is a large field beside the lane having the same name.

The local here is the **New Inn**, clearly a name telling us it is the more recent establishment even though it is not a particularly imaginative one.

# Halford

This name has been corrupted over the centuries, the first element slurred to hide its true meaning. Fortunately the image of Saxon life is preserved in records such as *Hauerford* 1155, and *Hawkeford* in 1535. This second record shows the origin of 'hawker's ford' well. However much we would like to see this as an image of a falconer exercising his bird alongside a river crossing, it is more likely that the name refers to a point where traders regularly forded the stream as they travelled the county selling their wares.

# Hampton

The only record of this name is from 1391 as *Hempton*. However this is sufficient to enable us to see that this place does not have the usual 'Hampton' definition of 'home farm' but this refers to 'the high farmstead', referring to its location above the Severn.

# Hampton Loade

The local here is the **Unicorn Inn**, a name found fairly regularly throughout the land. A fabled beast which is instantly recognised and, when it comes to pub names, is always heraldic. The most common reference is to Scotland. However, it also appears in the coat of arms of trades such as Chandlers, Goldsmiths and Apothecaries. Any of these may be relevant to this pub, for unless we know when we have no idea who it refers to, and it is difficult to understand why.

# Harley

Not as common a place name as one would expect. Once thought to refer to 'woodland clearing where hares were seen', the form of *Harlege* in Domesday (and later) hardly supports this. The true origin is Old English *haer* + *leah* '(place at) the rocky woodland clearing'. This may well have referred to one or two noticeable boulders rather than land which was littered with smaller stones and rocks.

The local pub is the **Plume of Feathers**. Here it refers to three ostrich feathers featured as the crest of Arthur, Prince of Wales and elder brother of the future Henry VIII. He was married to Catherine of Aragon when he died in 1502. His younger brother's later marriage to his widow lead to one of the most famous periods in English history.

# Hatton

A common place name and usually found in combination with an addition for distinction. Indeed that is the case in Shropshire, where there are two Hattons. The basic name is derived from Old English *haeth* + *tun*, giving 'the farmstead on a heath'.

Records of these places are as *Hatune* and *Hetune* in Domesday, as *Colde Hatton* in 1223, and as *Heye Hatton* in 1327. **Cold Hatton**'s addition comes from Old English *cald* literally meaning 'cold, exposed', and a good description of its position two miles southeast of **High Hatton** where the addition is *heah*, an Old English word meaning 'high' in the sense of 'chief' and having greater importance or standing.

# Haughton

There are three Haughtons in Shropshire. That near Shrewsbury is listed in Domesday as *Haustone*, however the similarly named place near Shifnal appears in the same record as *Halghton*, while that near Oswestry is recorded as *Halchton* in 1285. Three similar but significantly different records of names which not only have identical modern forms, but have identical origins. This name is from the Old English *halh* + *tun* or 'the farmstead on or by the nook of land'.

# Heath

Listed as *Hethe* in 1237 and *La Hethe* in 1267, this is exactly the same as every other place named such in England. With its origins in *haeth* it refers to '(the place at) the heath'.

Locally we find **Upper Norncott** and **Lower Norncott**, which is derived from *north mann cot* and telling us of 'the cottages of the northerners'. This name is a little misleading as these people were simply those living at the northern edge of the heathland. **Harp Coppice** and **Harp Farm** obviously have a common origin. This may be seen on a map dated 1846 where two adjacent fields produce an obvious triangular or harp shape, no trees are marked on the map yet this may simply be an oversight by the cartographer.

**Peckledy** is an unusual name, the only likely origin being a local mispronunciation of 'speckled' as 'peckled' with reference to the appearance of the land. The name of **Lower Tipping Yeld** and **Upper Tipping Yeld** are derived from *helde* or 'slope', with the element 'tipping' thought to have been a method of catching rabbits.

# Henley

A name found several times, especially in the central regions. Most of these are derived from Old English *heah* + *leah* 'the high woodland clearing', high being used in the sense of 'chief'. However, the three early forms of this name are indicators that Shropshire's Henley has a different first element. Listings of *Haneleu* in 1086, *Hennele* in 1242, and *Henneleg* in 1255, this Saxon name is from *henn* + *leah* '(place at) the woodland clearing frequented by the hens of wild birds'.

# Highley

The modern form is somewhat corrupted and has become so comparatively recently, as shown by the listings of *Hugelei* in Domesday, *Hugeleg* in 1242, and *Huggeleye* in 1291. Thus the first element is not describing 'high', however neither is it 'huge' as it would seem but is a personal name with the suffix *leah*. Highley comes from the Saxon telling of '(the settlement of) Hugga in the woodland clearing'.

**Silverdale Terrace** was formerly known as Long Row, a name by which some of the more senior residents still know the place. When the houses were built they were for the miners working at the local colliery. Not being trained miners, the colliery brought in experts from Newcastle-under-Lyme in Staffordshire who were working at the Silverdale Colliery, hence the name. Another unofficial name has been given to the Orchard, which was a grassy play area for children created in the 1960s. Prior to this there was a mass of fruit trees here, the reason for the name, which may well have provided greater entertainment for the children, albeit seasonally. **Coronation Street** was developed in 1901 and named in honour of the coronation of Edward VII.

The **Malt Shovel Inn** has a name which takes its name from the item used to turn the ingredients in the brewing process. Doubtless the earliest of inns having these names displayed an actual malt shovel, likely one which was no longer in use. Dennis Bache served the community as a local councillor. When he was growing up his family ran the New Inn in Highley. Later, when it was bought by Davenports Brewery, they decided they already had enough pubs of this name and decided to rename it **The Bache Arms** in honour of the former landlords.

# Hinstock

Domesday's record of this place is simply as *Stoche* in 1086. However almost two centuries later in 1242 we find the record of *Hinestok*. Here is another of the hybrid names, although the two languages here are not the normal Saxon and Scandinavian. In fact here we find Old English *stoc* together with the later Middle English *hine*, together telling us of 'the outlying or dependent settlement of the household servants'.

# Hints

There are only two places of this name in England; the other is in Staffordshire on the A5 trunk road. This name comes from a word related to Welsh *hynt* telling us this is '(the place at) the roads or paths'. Clearly the namesake refers to its position on the A5 or Watling Street, a well-known Roman road.

However, there is no major road at Hints in Shropshire, the closest being the A4117 which hardly qualifies as a major route. Perhaps the suggestion here is a meeting or crossroads where a number of routes converge, although modern maps do not confirm this. In fact no record that we know of could be perceived as giving weight to this definition, yet the origins are certain. Thus there are two possible explanations; either the people migrated here from a place where the name was better suited, and any notion as to where this place was is lost in history, or the name refers to paths or tracks rather than substantial roadways and is therefore probably much older than Saxon. Both of these explanations are plausible, yet will remain impossible to prove.

# Hodnet

A name recorded as *Hodenet* and *Odenet* in the eleventh century and as *Hodenet* and the modern form *Hodnet* in the early thirteenth century. In truth this name is much older, being British, originally given to the location and latterly taken for the name of the settlement. Two elements here, which can be seen to have become Welsh *hawdd* and *nant*, come together to tell us this is 'the pleasant valley'.

# Holdgate

A name of very different origins. This is no Saxon or Scandinavian name, nor is it earlier British but comes from a time following the Norman Conquest. Domesday records this place as *Stantune* an Old English name meaning 'the stony farmstead', or perhaps we should understand this more as 'the farmstead at the stone'. The lack of any other forms and the unreliability of Domesday make defining this name difficult. Yet clearly *Stantune* has no resemblance to Holdgate, so why the change? Other listings from later years provide the answer.

By 1185 we find this name recorded as *castellum Hologoti*, in 1242 as *Castrum Holegot*, in 1277 *Castrum de Holegot*, and by 1327 had been cut to simply *Holgod* and from then on to the modern form. In order to discover where this name comes from we have to refer again to Domesday. This great census of 1086 says the settlement of *Stantune* was held by a landlord by the name of Helgot. While this is an Old French name, the unreliability of Domesday when it comes to proper names may mean this is simply their version of the Old German names *Helgaud* or *Hildegaud* – we shall never know. However what we do know is that this Helgot was the basis of the modern name, the earlier records also showing Latin *castrum* and Middle English *castel* for the 'castle' which is now lost.

Local names here include **Brookhampton**, a name from Old English *broc-ham-tun* 'the brook home farmstead'. The brook spoken of is one of the headwaters of Trow Brook, which is defined under its own entry. There is also the name of **Castlemoor**, which is applied to a stretch of wet ground straddling the boundary between Holdgate, Tugford and Abdon. Thus this is likely a shortened version of Castle-Holdgate-Moor and referring to land which was equally claimed and otherwise ignored as unusable by all three places. A listing from 1274 refers to the place as *Ernesto Mora*, which shows it was then claimed by Earnstrey in adjoining Abdon.

# Hope

A common place name element, found as often in combination as it is alone, as it is here where the earliest record is as the modern form and dating from 1242. It comes from the Old English *hop* meaning 'a small enclosed valley'.

# Hope Bowdler

Under 9 miles south-east of Hope, this place has some rather interesting early listings. We have Domesday's *Fordritishope*, *Hop* and *Hope* from 1201, *Hopebulers* from 1273, and two years later *Hopbolers*. The prefix of the eleventh-century record is from an Old English personal name Forthraed, referring to the man who was leader of this settlement. The later addition is to commemorate the holding of this place by the de Bulers family, lords of this manor by 1201.

Locally we find **Chelmick** or 'Ceolmund's dairy farm'; **Ragdon**, from Middle English *ragge* and Old English *dun*, 'the hill of rough stone' which is a reminder of the quarries near here while **Copper Hole** recalls that this valuable metal was mined here. **Cwms Farm** is a name which comes from Old English *cumb* and previously known as *The Coomes* it means 'the short valley'. Apparently someone once thought it a good idea to use the Welsh spelling although it does not change the meaning.

**Whistlement** is a strange combination of *mynd* and *twisla*, telling us it was the 'rise by a road junction'.

# Hopton

There are six places in England with Hopton as, or at least part of, the name – and four are in Shropshire. Each is dealt with separately as they cannot really be considered to be particularly near to one another. The place known as simply Hopton, near Hodnet, is listed as *Hoptune* in Domesday and as *Hopton* as early as 1242. All of these places originate from the same Old English *hop* + *tun* 'the farmstead in an enclosed valley'.

# Hopton Cangeford

Records of *Hopton* in 1242 and *Hopton Cangefot* in 1242 show this to have identical origins with the former place of 'farmstead in an enclosed valley'. The addition here tells of the early possession by the Cangefot family, lords of the manor from at least the thirteenth century.

# Hopton Castle

Another 'farmstead in an enclosed valley' (see Hopton) recorded as *Opetune* in 1086. The addition, somewhat predictably, refers to the Norman castle which was erected here.

# Hopton Wafers

Listed as *Hopton* in Domesday and as *Hopton Wafre* in 1236, this fourth example of 'the farmstead in an enclosed valley' takes its distinguishing affix from the Wafre family. This manorial family certainly had possession by the thirteenth century, although it seems likely these French lords of the manor were here closer to the beginning of the previous century.

# Hordley

From records such as *Hordelei* 1086, *Hordeleg* 1242, and *Hordileg* 1255, we can see this to be from Old English *hord* + *leah*. An intriguing definition here for this name means '(the settlement) at the woodland clearing where treasure was found'. There are no records of any treasure trove being found here, other than the usual collection of odd coins and other artefacts which are found at all settlements with any longevity. Thus the name suggests two possibilities. Either a substantial treasure horde was found here and soon disposed of somehow, or the find is an exaggeration and represents a find of limited value. The most plausible is a crock of coins (possibly Roman) which was unearthed during the earliest days of building here. The find would have been of little historical value and the settlers would have arranged to dispose of them for (what they would have considered) suitable trade.

# Horton

A common name and found throughout England as both minor names and also given to whole settlements. This place near Wem is listed as *Hortune* from Old English *horu* + *tun* which, along with the majority of these places, is derived from 'the dirty or muddy farmstead'.

The **Queens Head** is a common enough name for a public house, often depicting the image of Queen Elizabeth I but only because hers is one of the most easily recognised image apart from her namesake and living monarchs are not considered.

# Howle

With early records of this name as *Hugle* and *Hulam* from 1086 and 1253 respectively, we can see this to be derived from Old English *hugol*. Rarely found on its own, this name tells us of '(the place at) the mound of earth or hillock'.

# Hughey

All of the information we require regarding the origins of this name date from the thirteenth century, indeed from the very beginning and the end of that period in history. The first record of this name is as *Leg* in 1203. This is clearly from Old English *leah* and refers to '(the place at) the woodland clearing'. This same document also speaks of this manor being held by one Hugh. By the time the next record is found as *Huleye* in 1291 the place has become '(the place at) Hugh's woodland clearing'.

Here we find the **Hughley Brook** which was named from the place. Records of this name from 1607 show it as *Plaish Brook* (see under Plaish) and also simply *Ree*. This latter name is a Middle English *atter ee* simply meaning 'at the river', the loss of most of *atter* is not unknown in place names. Further down this tributary it is known as Harley Brook, another example of back-formation from the name of Harley, yet in the modern era very unusual to find two names for the same river.

**Ippikins Rock** in 1842 is labelled *Hipkins Rock Piece* which shows the modern form is an odd corruption of what was originally a personal name. Other individuals are commemorated by **Grandmother's Meadow** and the oddly named field of **Titty Finch**.

# I

## Ifton Heath

The sole record of this name is as *Iftone* from 1272. Such a dearth of examples makes defining the name with any certainty extremely difficult. However it seems the basic name is that of an individual with Old English *tun*, giving us 'the farmstead of a man called Ifa'. The additional 'Heath' is self-explanatory and is likely a local name which has come to the fore.

## Ightfield

With records of *Istefelt* in 1086, *Hichtefeld* in 1175, *Ihttefeld* in 1230, and *Ihtenefeld* in 1260, this is from the Old English *feld* and gives us '(place at) the open land by the River Ight'. This is a British river-name of uncertain origins, although there has been a suggestion that this is something seen today as Welsh *eithin* 'furze', whereby we would expect to find this plant along the river somewhere.

## Ironbridge

A very late name, coined to describe the world's first bridge constructed from iron and which opened in 1779.

Local pubs have names with a more subtle message, such as the **Malt House** which is a reference to the brewing process and a name which brings to mind the promise of a drink. Similarly, but for a completely different reason, **Ye Olde Robin Hood** would be seen to be a pub because of being described as 'ye olde', an addition which does not always mean the place is particularly ancient but is used to indicate a public house. No explanation of Robin Hood's story is required, the character is known across the globe. His fame is the reason for his name being found so far from his traditional home of Sherwood in Nottinghamshire. The reference is almost certainly to the Ancient Order of Foresters which, founded in 1834, is a friendly society which were opening new courts and lodges throughout the nineteenth century. The sign showed the pub as a meeting place for the order, which was mistakenly said to be a depiction of Robin Hood.

Enabling sign painters to depict a pleasing or welcoming aspect or scene soon became a factor in the choice of name. It is not simply the subject matter which is important but how it is described. For example, to call a pub 'Grassland' or 'Farmland' would not be particularly attractive to customers, however the **Meadow Inn** conjures up an image of serenity where grazing animals are seen amid the lush grass and wild flowers. An alternative name may be 'Paddock', a term associated with an area for horses and also used to describe the place where the **Horse & Jockey** are united prior to the start of a horse race.

A most unique name is found opposite the bridge which gives the place its name. The **Tontine Hotel** ultimately derives its name from an Italian banker, Lorenzo Tonti who died in 1684, ninety-one years before the bridge was started. He was the first financier to suggest a system of investment in a project where the return was higher for the lifetime of the investor but all claims on the share issue died with him. The shares were then distributed equally between the surviving investors. This process continued until the sole survivor died and no further monies were payable. This system, named after the banker, funded the building of the bridge and gave name to the hotel which faces it.

*The span of the famous bridge at Ironbridge.*

# K

## Kemberton

A name found in Domesday as *Chenbritone* and as *Kembricton* in 1242. This is a name derived from Old English, the personal name being followed by *tun*. Here we find this to be 'the farmstead of a man named Cenbeorht'.

Regulars at the **Masons Arms** today would be unlikely to recognise the coat of arms granted to the Company of Masons in 1473. At Kemberton it would be unlikely to have been an indication of a meeting place for such skilled workers. It was probably opened by someone who had previously been associated with the builder's trade.

## Kempton

This place near Clun is listed as *Chenipitune* in 1086 and *Kempeton* in 1256. Another name of Old English derivation, although there is some uncertainty as to the first element. If the origins are *cempa* + *tun* then this is 'farmstead of the warrior'. However the first element may be the name of an individual, in which case this is 'Cempa's farmstead'. If the latter is the case, this would be a nickname of the same meaning.

## Kenley

Records of *Chenelie* 1086, *Kemelee* 1203, *Kenele* 1219, and *Keneleg* 1228 point to a name of Saxon or Old English derivation. Here the personal name is followed by *leah*, giving '(place at) the woodland clearing of a man called Cena'.

# Kenwick

The same personal name is seen here as in the previous place. However this does not mean it is by any means the same person. Indeed the two places are almost as far as it is possible to be within the county, this is simply a fairly common personal name.

Listed in 1203 as *Kenewic*, this is an Old English name with the suffix *wic*. Here we find 'the specialised farm of a man called Cena' – almost invariably the speciality referred to was as a dairy farm.

# Ketley

Early records of this name are found as *Cattelega* 1177, *Ketel* 1200, *Kettelea* 1255, and *Kettley* 1679. These forms differ somewhat, making it difficult to see what the first element may be here. The twelfth-century record could suggest a personal name of Catta or Cyt, yet these are difficult to see evolving to become Ket and thus we must opt for a different origin. Thus the first word may be either *cyta* or *cyte* suffixed by *leah* giving 'woodland clearing where kites are seen' and 'cottage or cell in a woodland clearing' respectively.

Minor names here include **Cow Wood**, formerly known as Gorsty Wood until the collier's cottages were built here. Thus it is thought that this name comes from the dialect word *cow* meaning 'coal'.

**Pottersbank** is the only remaining sign of the potters who were here in 1763 but had disappeared fifty years later.

Not every lake is what it seems, for example the **Redlake** is not a lake at all but a Saxon *lacu* – however the colour is correct and speaks of 'the red drainage channel'.

While the **Shoulder of Mutton** has been used as a pub name throughout the land, it is not always derived from the eighteenth-century delicacy served with cucumber sauce. Sometimes it comes from where it stands, such as a field name which describes its shape being reminiscent of this cut of meat.

# Kinlet

Early records of this name have been found as *Chinlete* 1086, *Kinleet* 1185, and *Kinlet* in 1201. Here it is an Old English or Saxon name from *cyne* + *hlet*, which describes 'the royal share or lot'. This definition is a direct reference to this manor being held by Queen Edith, widow of Edward the Confessor, in 1066.

Note that any official reference in a Norman record to the earlier Saxon king (notably Domesday) is to Edward the Confessor. Despite Harold II being regarded as the ruler of England by the English in 1066, his claim to the throne was not recognised in France, hence the invasion.

# Kinnerley

An Old English personal name followed by *leah*, telling us this was 'Cyneheard's woodland clearing' and is identical to the very similar Kinnersley in Worcestershire. Early forms of this name include *Chenardelei* 1086 and *Kinardeslegh* in 1223.

# Knockin

A very unusual-sounding name for a place, this is entirely due to its origins. The earliest record of this place is as *Cnochin* in 1165, with *Cnukin* in 1196, *Knokyn* in 1197, and *Knukin* in 1198. That the first record known dates from 1165 is misleading, for the name is much older than this. Coming from a Celtic word *cnoccin*, which is related to Welsh *cnycyn*, this refers to 'a little hillock'. Clearly this name applied to the locality prior to the settlement ever appearing, which explains the records only existing in the twelfth century.

*Knockin Seat, erected to mark the Golden Jubilee of Queen Victoria, 24 June 1887.*

# L

## Lawley

A name found as *Lavelei* in Domesday in 1086 and as *Laueleye* in 1285. These are clear indications of this name being derived from a Saxon personal name with Old English *leah*, which gives 'Lafa's woodland clearing'.

One field name found here is a common one, not always seen as coming from Old English. Here **The Yelds** comes from *helde* which speaks of a 'gentle slope'.

## Leaton

There are few records of this place which can aid us in defining this name. With only Domesday's *Letone* and *Leton* from 1212, we can see the suffix as Old English *tun* but the first element is uncertain. Two different elements have been suggested, either *hleo* which would give 'shelter at the farmstead', or *laet* which would give 'the water course at the farmstead'.

Hereabouts we find the region known as **The Corner**; a sharp feature produced when new houses were built in about 1900 and unknown prior to this. **The Dingle** is a stream name running south from the church and means just that, probably the closest modern term would be 'rivulet'. It is also recorded as **Leaton Dingle** and **Dunns Dingle**, the latter name also seen as **Dunn's Heath** and recalling a family who lived around here for several generations.

## Lee

Although there is only one listing of this name, exactly as the modern form in 1327, there is no doubt as to its origins. This place comes from a very commonly found Old English element *leah* meaning 'woodland clearing'. What is unusual is to find this element alone; it is only used with another element as a suffix.

# Lee Brockhurst

As with the previous place, this is from the Old English *leah* and speaks of the '(place at) the woodland clearing'. With about only 7 miles between the two, a second element is to be expected, although this is not found in Domesday's *Lege*. We have to wait until 1285 when the place is seen as *Leye under Brochurst*. The addition is also Saxon, from *brocc* + *hyrst*, giving 'the wooded hill frequented by badgers'. From the record of the thirteenth century we can see that this was originally two places. The most likely explanation is that the two began life very close together and, as they grew in size, the boundaries merged.

# Leebotwood

Domesday records this place simply as *Botewde*, and not until 1170 do we find anything like the modern form in *Lega in Bottewode*. Clearly from these records we can see the original name was simply a Saxon personal name with Old English *wudu*. Later there is an addition from *leah*. Just why this addition came to be is a mystery. We have no knowledge of any secondary settlement, so we have to discount any similar 'joining' as is seen with Lee Brockhurst. The only explanation we can offer with the clues we have is that the vast majority of woodland settlements were founded in clearings, thus his form was simply expected. Therefore this fairly unique name can be defined as the '(place at) the clearing in the wood of Botta'.

# Leighton

A handful of Leightons in England, yet Shropshire's version is the only one without an addition. There is no doubt this is Old English in origin form *leac* + *tun*. Listed as *Lestone* in Domesday, *Leocton* in 1188, and *Lecton* in 1198, this is 'the leek or garlic enclosure'. This is somewhat specific and some understand this may communicate something more akin to a 'herb garden'.

The **Kynnersley Arms** marks the name of the neighbouring village.

# Lilleshall

Some very old and quite different listings of this place, including *Lilsaetna gemaere* in 963, *Linleshelle* 1086, *Lilleshull* 1162, and *Lilleshell* 1200. Here we find a Saxon personal name with Old English *hyll* and giving us '(place at) the hill of a man called Lill'. Here Lilleshall Abbey gave its name to **Abbey Bridge**, **Abbey Wood** and **Abbey Farm**.

A glance at the map will reveal there are two very distinct periods when names developed here, in the early days of the settlement and at the onset of the Industrial Revolution. The earlier Saxon times gave us the very similar **Donnington** 'Dunna's farmstead' and **Honington** or 'Hunna's farmstead', with **Muxton** being 'Mucel's farmstead'. **Lamy Lakes** is an early field name, coming from *lamig* it speaks of the 'loamy' soil at the *lacu* or 'boundary stream'.

The name of **Lubstree Park** is an interesting one, for despite records of **Lubstry Poole**, **Luvstye Meadow**, and **Lopstree Moor** it seems the first 'L' is erroneous. Clearly this originally applied to just one name, although none of these examples was the first, for Old English *up stig* refers to the 'upland path'. This is a road which runs along slightly raised ground along the edge of the Weald Moors, bordering all these places.

Another name with several examples comes from an obvious personal name. **Phillips Acre** speaks for itself, as does **Phillips Yard**, while **Phillips Pingle** is from *pightel* ' a small enclosure', and **Phillips Stew** points to the location of a fish pond where carp were raised as food fish.

*Lilleshall's thirteenth-century Augustinian Abbey.*

Later names include **Waxhill Houses** which tells us that beeswax was either found or perhaps produced here. **Pains Lane**, which was to become **St George's Lane**, led to the chapel. Yet dates show the later name did not exist before the place of worship, thus Pain must be a family name.

A map dated 1220 shows the name of *Holebroc*, which comes from Old English *hol broc* or 'the brook in the hollow'. However today this is shown as **Humber Brook**, a name also seen nearby in **The Humbers** and **Humber Arm**. In 1580 we find a reference to *Mr Lusons Hammers*, water-driven hammers used in the making of iron and owned by a Walter Leveson. This is one of the very few occasions when a piece of technology gave names to a field, a river and even an arm of the Shropshire canal.

The local here is the **Red House Inn**, a name where the etymology is obvious to anyone who has seen it. The place is quite clearly very red and stands out in the landscape.

# Linley

There are two places of this name in Shropshire, although it is found throughout England as a minor place name. This one near Bridgnorth is recorded as *Linlega* in 1135 and *Lindleg* in 1204. Both have identical origins in Old English *lind + leah* or '(the place at) the clearing in the wood of lime trees'.

This Linley has local names such as **Caughley** or 'the woodland glade where jackdaws are seen', although this may have been a personal name Ceahha, which is also the word for a jackdaw.

The name of **Darley** is from *deor leah* 'the woodland clearing where deer are seen'.

**Hem** takes its name from the position of the house on the southern boundary of the parish. **Hifnal** from *hufe cnyll* speaks of the 'hood-shaped hillock'.

The small 'strip of woodland' alongside Dean Brook is known as **Devil's Den**, while **Swinney** might mean 'swine island' but is no island as we would know, it refers to slightly raised ground near the Severn.

The name of the **Ragleth** public house comes from Ragleth Hill to the east of the village, the name telling us this is the 'hill where *ragu* or lichen is seen'.

# Linley

A small settlement near Norbury, this place is listed as *Linlega* in about 1150 and *Lindele* in 1209, it has identical origins to the previous name '(the place at) the clearing in the wood of lime trees'.

# Little Stretton

As with All Stretton and Church Stretton, this name comes from Old English *straet* + *tun* and is 'the farmstead on the Roman road'. Clearly this addition is to differentiate from the two larger like-named places in the county.

Here we find **Minton**, 'the settlement by the Mynd'; **Ragleth Hill** speaks of 'the rough stone on the concave hill'; **Wiresytch** is clearly 'the small stream by a weir'; **Wernshin** is a Welsh name speaking of 'the alder tree swamp', while **Queensbatch Mill** is *cwene baece*, 'the woman's stream valley', with the mill first seen named in 1392.

*The thatched church of All Saints' at Little Stretton.*

# Llanfair Waterdine

If there was ever any clue as to Shropshire's border with Wales, this name demonstrates it perfectly. Indeed it comes as no surprise to find this place is virtually on that border and has its origins in that Celtic tongue.

Records of this place are quite numerous, as *Watredene* 1086, *Waterdene* 1278, *Thlanveyr* 1284, and *Llanver* 1560. Clearly there are two distinct names here, both of which are represented in that found in the twenty-first century. The first element is from Welsh *llan* meaning 'church' and a mutated *Mair* which refers to the saint to whom said church is dedicated. The addition is from the Old English or Saxon language. Here *waeter* + *denu* is added and gives us a rather lengthy definition of 'the church of St Mary in the watery (or wet) valley'.

# Llanyblodwel

While the previous name is more easily seen as a Welsh and English hybrid, this may seem to be wholly from the former language. However appearances (or even sounds) can be deceptive, the records of *Blodwelle* in about 1200 and *Llanblodwell* in 1535 show this is another Welsh and English combination.

As with the previous name the first element is Welsh *llan*, which would normally given this as 'the church of Blodwell'. However there is no such saint and the early record at the beginning of the thirteenth century points to this being an earlier place name. Indeed the origin here is Old English *blod* + *wella* which, when combined with the later addition, gives an origin of 'the church by the blood-coloured stream'. This seemingly rather macabre name most likely refers to the stream being coloured by a natural suspension. However there are some sources which suggest the 'blood' may be a remnant of local superstition.

## Llanymynech

In 1254 this place is recorded as *Llanemeneych* and in 1282 as *Llanymeneich*. This is wholly a Welsh name from *llan* + *mynach* or 'the church of the monks'.

## Longden

Even without Domesday's record of *Langedune* and that of *Longedun* from 1236, this is clearly the Old English *lang* + *dun* or 'the long hill'. As with other places it seems likely that this name was given to the area at an early date and later taken by the settlement.

The local pub is the **Tankerville Arms**, named after the Earl of Tankerville, a peerage created three times, (1418, 1695 and 1714), because the line became extinct twice and which may well happen for a third time as there is currently no heir apparent to the title. Prior to 1867 it was known as the Tankerville Inn. The name was changed following a shocking murder which made national headlines. Catherine Lewis was staying at the inn three days before Christmas 1867 when she was brutally murdered. The post-mortem of the nine-year-old girl was held on the premises – a common occurrence at the time. Three days later John Mapp was arrested and imprisoned awaiting trial. The thirty-five-year-old had been back in Longden for eighteen months. In 1859 he had been transported to Australia as punishment for attacking an old woman. In March of 1868 Mapp was found guilty, the judge sentencing him to be hanged and afterwards to be buried within the confines of the prison grounds. His victim was buried in the churchyard of St Ruthen's, even though Catherine Lewis was not a member of the congregation.

# Longdon upon Tern

This place cannot be considered to be close to the previous place, there being at least 15 miles between them. Thus the addition must be because of the number of 'long hills' as a minor place name. The addition is, as discussed under Eaton upon Tern, a Celtic river name meaning 'the strong one'.

*The 'fast-flowing' Tern at Longdon on Tern.*

# Longford

There are two places in Shropshire with this name. One near Market Drayton is recorded as *Langeford* in the thirteenth century, while its namesake near Newport is found as *Langanford* and *Langeford* in 1002 and 1086 respectively.

It hardly seems necessary to give this as '(place at) the long ford', coming from the almost as obvious Old English *lang* + *ford*. However the term 'long' may need some explanation. The reference may be understood to be a ford across a wide stream, i.e. a 'long' distance to be travelled. While there are doubtless places where this is applicable, normally we would find the broader the river or stream, the deeper the central portion and thus a stronger current making fording the river an unwise thing to attempt. The vast majority of these names would refer to a place where the river was capable of being forded along a lengthy portion of the banks.

# Longnor

Few early listings of this name, as *Longenalra* in 1170 and as *Longenolre* in 1333, making this name a little difficult to understand. There is little doubt the basic Old

English here is *lang* and *alor*. However just what sense these early forms convey depends upon which record we favour as the more accurate, or indeed how we look at it. The obvious derivation to give is '(place at) the long alder copse', yet this has a distinctly impractical feel to it. In order to qualify as a copse there should be a minimum of six tightly packed trees. Alders are not often seen too close together in such numbers and, the major point here, the 'long' copse hardly makes sense unless these were not from a natural seeding. Therefore it is possible that it refers to a noticeably tall alder, or one which stood out in an area where much shorter trees prevailed. Thus the alternative would be '(place at) the tall alder tree'.

## Longville in the Dale

There is no doubt this comes from two Old English words *lang* + *feld* or 'the long open space', as shown by records such as *Longefewd* in 1255 and *Longfeld* in 1291. What is unusual is that Saxon *feld* evolved to become 'ville', which is more of an American place name than anything found in England. Indeed the colonies may well have influenced this place for the form is particularly late.

This recent change is also true of the addition. It certainly comes from *dael* or 'valley' but does not get a mention in the earliest forms. However the origins are indeed from Saxon times and it seems likely that this was a name used locally for many years before it ever appeared on any map.

## Loppington

As soon as the trained eye sees a place name with 'ing' they will know the previous element will be a personal name. There are a very few exceptions to this rule, however all are corruptions and have no basis from the Old English element *inga*.

Loppington is recorded as *Lopitune* in 1086, *Lopinton* in 1199, and *Lopington* in 1230. This is from a Saxon personal name followed by *inga* and *tun* and telling us this was once 'the farmstead of the family or followers of Loppa'.

Loppington Hall was the home of Lieutenant-Colonel John Lloyd Dickin and his father Major Thomas Dickin J.P, D.L., who were particularly influential in India during the days of the British Empire. However, John also served in Canada, Malta, New Zealand, Australia and Baluchistan, learning the Russian language and joining Sir Martin Conway's expedition to the Karakoram Himalayas in 1892. The influential family are remembered in the name of the local pub, the **Dickin Arms**.

# Loughton

From 1138 comes the record of *Lukintone* which is followed by *Luhtune* in 1225. Undoubtedly this features the Old English *luh + tun* and is 'the farmstead near the pool'. This may not seem a particularly distinctive name for a place, for all farms obviously needed some water supply for their crops and/or livestock. This may indicate there was once another element to this name which has been lost – most likely an adjective describing the pool.

# Ludford

The only record of note is that of *Ludeford* in Domesday. This comes from Old English *hlude + ford* describing the 'river crossing on the noisy stream'. The stream in question is the River Teme, while the reference to 'noise' is somewhat misleading. Any noise is simply the tinkling of the waters through the shallows of the ford, the Teme being among the fastest rivers in the land.

The estate of Ludford Park was bought by the Charlton family in the seventeenth century, and they retained possession until 1920. Edmund Charlton built Ludford Lodge and Cliff Villas in the early nineteenth century. At the same time he constructed Steventon Villas at the top of Primrose Bank. Said to be a healthier location high above the wetland, it proved less popular after the outbreak of typhoid at the end of the nineteenth century. The family are remembered in the name of the local inn, the **Charlton Arms**.

# Ludlow

Exactly the same first element as the previous name, and for the same reasons, only here the suffix is Old English *hlaw*. This is 'the hill at the noisy stream', although it is possible the reference is to a tumulus on the hill for either is equally plausible. Early forms of this name are found as *Ludelaue* in 1138 and *Ludelawa* in 1177.

One of Ludlow's most famous landmarks is its castle. First built in the early twelfth century, it is now partially ruined but still dominates the town as it overlooks the Teme. Many stories have been told about a resident ghost, the most unusual dating from just after the First World War when more than fifty people heard the ghost, said to be emanating from within the castle walls themselves. A dog which was on the tour refused to move and the hair on its back bristled.

The place has long been said to be the haunt of two lovers. The mistress, one Marion de la Bruere, took the life of her lover Arnold de Lys. Confusion surrounds the reasons why she would have taken the life of the man she apparently loved, yet all report she plunged the sword repeatedly into his chest. His screams are still heard echoing around the old building each time the blade penetrates.

Part of the castle is known as Mortimer's Tower, this has given a name to **Tower Street**. Roger Mortimer enlarged the castle during the fourteenth century.

*Horseshoe Weir, Ludlow.*

The shell of what must have been a magnificent building for its day is what we see today. Such wonderful surroundings attracted notable visitors including royalty. Mary Tudor, often referred to as Bloody Mary, spent three winters at Ludlow Castle during her five-year reign, while Prince Arthur, elder brother of Henry VIII, honeymooned here shortly before his early death. His wife was none other than Catherine of Aragon, who was afterward to marry Henry and bring about one of the most written about times in English history. Aside from becoming the first of the famed six wives, their marriage led to England's break from the Catholic Church.

Formerly known as Parsons Lane, **College Street** is named after the Ludlow College, one of the oldest continuous educational establishments in Britain dating back over 800 years. **King Street**, which alludes to the builder of the castle, is known locally as The Narrows and certainly merits the name.

The river, a tributary of the Teme, has given its name to **Corve Street**, while **Harp Lane** takes its name from the inn of that name which stood at the eastern end of the street from 1746, when it was run by Francis and Mary Winwood. **Julian Road** and **St Julian's Avenue** are named after the holy well near here, which has always been associated with this saint. **Dodmore Lane** runs alongside the field where the parasitic plant dodder grew.

Local pubs take their names from a number of areas. The **Penny Black Inn** recalls the world's first ever postage stamp and undoubtedly the best known. The sign depicts the stamp and thus the head of Queen Victoria. The **Nelson Inn** is named in honour of England's greatest ever hero, indeed nobody has more pubs named after them than Lord Horatio Nelson. The **Compasses Inn** marks a connection with one of the trades, such as mason, carpenter, joiner, where this instrument was required much the same as it once was by any draughtsman, before the computer made the tool almost obsolete.

While many pubs called **Boot Inn** will have signs showing an assortment of reasons for the name, most notably the footwear made famous by the Duke of Wellington, the real origin is a basic one. This tough, durable footwear has always been associated with manual labour and would have been simple to show on a sign pointing to an establishment for the working classes. The **Raven Inn** features a bird appearing many times in folklore and history. Sacred to the Druids, mentioned by Shakespeare as fostering poor children, known by the Vikings as Woden's bird, and claimed to be how King Arthur maintains an eternal vigil over his kingdom, the true reference as a pub name is probably political. The name never appears to have been popular before the seventeenth century, when it was adopted by Jacobite sympathisers to show allegiance by the innkeeper and/or his customers. The **Bennetts End Inn** comes initially from a field to the east of Ludlow, itself referring to a former occupant. The name was later given to Bennetts End Cottage and from there to the pub.

# Lydbury North

While the same element is seen here as in the preceding two names, its use is rather different. Records of *Lideberie* in 1086, *Lindeberinort* 1167, *Leddebur* in 1212, and *Liddebury North* in 1223 show the addition was an early one, although there are no other Lydburys close by or anywhere else. It is thought that the addition was to distinguish between this and Ledbury, which has a completely different meaning and origin.

This name tells us of 'the stronghold by the stream known as Hlyde'. As we have already seen this is an Old English name meaning 'the noisy one', although here it refers to an unrelated watercourse.

The **Powis Arms** is a local which refers to the title created three times over the centuries, each resurrection because the previous line had become extinct. Firstly in 1674 for William Herbert, secondly in 1748 for Henry Arthur Herbert who had married the niece of the last holder of the title, and lastly Edward Clive, an ancestor of Robert Clive of India. The title has always been associated with the position of Lord Lieutenant of Shropshire.

# Lydham

Early records of this name are clearly of different spellings, yet the pronunciation is identical. In Domesday this is found as *Lidum*, by 1250 this has become *Lideham*, and seventeen years later as *Lidun*. Here the origin is Old English *hlid* referring to '(place at) the gates or slopes'.

# M

## Madeley

A name also found in nearby Staffordshire and has the same meaning. This name is from a Saxon personal name with Old English *leah* and telling us it was 'Mada's woodland clearing'. Some sources suggest that Mada is a nickname and refers to someone regarded as 'foolish'. However whether this is correct and just what gave them such a reputation will never be known. The early records of this place are as *Madelie* in 1086 and *Madelega Prioris* in 1167, the latter referring to religious connections and used simply to distinguish from namesakes across the border in Staffordshire.

**Mad Brook** is a shortened version of Madeley Brook, a process known as back-formation where the river is named from the place rather than the normal way around.

**Blists Hill**, a famous name in the early days of iron smelting, is commonly quoted as being a corruption of 'blast' as in furnace. However the name is found well before then and it must come from a personal name.

Other names of note include **Brock Holes** which is derived from *brocc hol* and speaks of the 'badger setts', **Strethill Farm** 'the tongue of land', while **Whales Back** is the name of a small hill of a shape reminiscent of this huge mammal seen surfacing.

**Victoria Road** was previously known as Bridle Road, where horses were walked, and earlier still as Shooting Butts, where archery targets were set up for practice. The modern name was given in honour of Britain's longest-serving monarch.

Names are sometimes not what they seem, such as **Cripples Hill** which takes its name from Old English *crypel* referring to a 'burrow' or 'narrow passage'. However, many names do state the obvious such as **Bedlam Cottages**; built near the furnaces by Madeley Wood they are indeed a reference to the noise!

The names of the local pubs are from a number of different sources, none more unusual than the **All Nations Inn**. Although there is a clear message that everyone is welcome, this is secondary from the true origin. Until two hundred years ago the phrase was used to speak of 'a mixture', in pub parlance a concoction made from all the unfinished bottles. The **Beacon** is close to where a signal fire is lit in order to announce an important event. Once it was the fastest way to announce the birth or death of a royal or even of invasion, today it is symbolic. Often names such as the **Hungry Horse** have been created to advertise the food being served, while alluding to the times when the horse was the only means of transport. As mentioned there were furnaces here near the wood, hence the name of the **Three Furnaces**.

# Maesbrook

This place name is recorded in Domesday as *Meresbroc* and *Maysbrok* in 1272. As discussed in the introduction any proper name in this great tome should be regarded with some degree of suspicion. Unfortunately these are the only records we have of this name, yet both suggest a different first element. The earlier record would point to Old English *maere* + *broc* which tells of '(place at) the brook of the boundary'. Indeed this place is very close to the border with Wales, so it is no surprise to find the Welsh *maes* with Old English *broc* suggested as an alternative. If this is the true origin the place would be defined as '(place at) the open field by the brook'.

It should be noted that the former definition is considered the more likely; however this may only be because of association with the following name. While the two places are only 3 miles apart, there appears to be no other connection.

The **Black Horse Inn** is often said to be heraldic, indeed it could be said to represent many different areas from the 7th Dragoon Guards to a high street bank, yet it can just as readily have been a view from the place or a favourite animal of the owner or innkeeper.

# Maesbury

From *Mereserie* in 1086 to *Mersburi* in 1272 there is no doubt this is from Old English *maere* + *burh* 'the stronghold near the boundary'.

The local pub has an unusual name with a very simple explanation. **The Original Ball** enabled the sign painter to produce a very simple and yet attractive sign, a major factor in deciding upon a pub name. However when another pub grew up nearby and took the same name, possibly because of the transfer of some individuals from one to the other, the addition of 'original' produced a unique name. Today the other Ball has gone.

# Marchamley

A name which has two equally plausible meanings. Records as *Marcemeslei* in 1086, *Merchemeslega* in 1185, and *Merchemlee* in 1206 do not help us to differentiate between the two. This may be 'woodland clearing of a man called Merchelm', the personal name being suffixed by the common Saxon element *leah*. However there is an equal possibility that the first element is a plural form of Saxon *Mierce* giving 'woodland clearing at the territory of the Mercians'. It seems unlikely that either of these will be shown to be the true origin with any certainty.

# Market Drayton

Drayton is one of the popular place names in England, always derived from Old English *draeg* + *tun* referring to a 'farmstead at or near a portage'. A portage was a number of things, such as a short stretch of marshland between two navigable stretches of water, but all involve dragging something over a short distance.

The listings for this name include *Draitune* in 1086. However, it was only comparatively recently (in the timescale of place names) that the additional Market was used to tell of this being the site of an important market.

Street names in this town represent its history, however there are fewer dignitaries and notable individuals than are normally found in a town with such a long history. **Frogmore Road** led through wetland, **Smithfield Road** was the site of the cattle market, while **Maer Lane** is a corruption of the Saxon *mere* or 'pond' which was also a name found on earlier maps. **Greenfields Lane** was formerly known as **Fat Farm Lane**, both of which suggest this place was highly productive farmland.

**Bishops Lane**, **Simons Road** and **Dalelands** took their names from the family of Mr Bishop, Mr Simon and John Dale respectively. **Clive Road** is named after Robert Clive (of India) with whom the town is closely associated. **Bert Smith Way** is named after the man who was the town's first mayor, appointed in 1974. Drayton's first secondary modern school was first run by the headmaster who is commemorated by **Llewellyn Roberts Way**. Despite much speculation, the individual associated with **Parker Bowles Drive** is one Eustace Parker Bowles, a JP who did much work for the community.

**Grotto Road** was formerly known as Pig Sty Lane and was changed to make it sound more agreeable.

After the Battle of Blore Heath in 1459 Lord Salisbury and his men camped on Salisbury Hill, **Salisbury Road** offers good views of the hill.

Shavington Hall was once the home of the Earls of Kilmorey, a part of the family crest gave a name to **Phoenix Bank**.

For one person to provide the names of two streets, they must be a major figure; indeed **Queen Street** and **Alexander Street** were named after the consort of Edward VII.

**Betton Road**, which is now named after the place which it connects with Drayton, was formerly known as **Jenny Trevor's Lane** and said to mark the lane where that poor woman was found hanged in the latter half of the nineteenth century. A unique street name, certainly from the name and possibly from the etymology, is **Pezenas Drive**. Named after the town in the south of France, it was given following the signing of the town-twinning agreement, itself the result of both being associated with Clive of India.

In the town is a building known as the **Red House** in Shropshire Street. This late eighteenth-century townhouse became the home of William Wilkinson, the master of the frigate *Sirius* at the Battle of Trafalgar in 1805. This vessel was the first to report to Admiral Nelson the approach of the enemy out of Cadiz and alerting them to the eventual battle.

The town seems always to have been associated with food and, in particular, styles itself 'the home of gingerbread'; there is even an inn named **The Gingerbread Man**.

The **Clive & Coffyne** recalls the town's most famous resident, Robert Clive, who was reputed to have brought back the recipe for the small pie to which the second half of the name refers.

Other pubs in the town include the **Sandbrook Vaults**, the name of the family who owned the pub for over a century from the beginning of the nineteenth century. The **Joiners Arms** displays that trade's coat of arms and shows an allegiance with that trade, possibly in the form of a former owner rather than a reference to the clientele.

*The Clive and Coffyne at Market Drayton.*

There are very few pubs named the **Stags Head Inn** which are not found on or near former hunting land. Those found elsewhere have some other connection with the hunt, either in a person or maybe a trophy found on the premises.

The sign at the **Lord Hill** commemorates the military career of the Right Honourable Rowland Lord Hill, Commander in Chief of the British Army. If anyone doubts the stature of this soldier in British history, take a look at his statue in Shrewsbury which is over 130ft high and is the largest doric statue in the world.

For many years the **Corbet Arms** was known as the Talbot Arms and was the centre for the manorial court. The Corbet family were lords of the manor for many years, some may even consider the family to still hold the title, while the steward of the estate held the title of mayor and was landlord of the Corbet Arms.

# Marsh

A very obvious name, from Old English *mersc* it infers '(the place at) the marsh'. However it is unusual to find this name on its own, usually the element appears as a suffix in a place name. Maybe this suggests this was not the original name of the place, but was formerly a minor place name. Without concrete evidence being found this will remain pure speculation.

# Melverley

Domesday's record of *Melevrlei* is the only record found until that of *Milverlegh* in 1311. The unreliability of the eleventh-century census is discussed in the introduction and the record from the fourteenth century is very little evidence for us to give a definition with any certainty. However, from what information we have it would appear this is Old English *myln* + *ford* + *leah* or '(place at) the woodland clearing near the mill ford'.

*An informative signpost at Melverley, also showing cycle routes.*

# Meole Brace

A name recorded in 1086 as simply *Melam*, which by 1203 had been reduced even further to *Mole*, *Moles* in 1210, *Meeles* in 1242, and something which can be seen as approaching the modern form in 1273 *Melesbracy*. This place probably takes its name from the Meole Brook, which is today known as the Rea Brook. The origin of the name Meole is uncertain, records being very scarce indeed. However it is possible this is from Old English *melu* used in a figurative sense to describe a stream with a high proportion of sediment by saying it is 'mealy'.

The addition is from the thirteenth-century lords of this manor, the de Braci family. There seems no apparent reason for a distinguishing addition, the nearest similar name is as far away as Merseyside. It is tempting to suggest this is further evidence of the basic name being common to both the settlement and its stream.

Today known as the **Rea Brook** the name has also been transferred to **Rea Cottages**, found from 1843. This is a Middle English term *atter ee* meaning 'at the river', a common name which always has the same origins. There is also the name of **Washford Farm** which comes from Old English *waesc - ford* meaning 'the west ford' and refers to the direction in which the current flows.

**Newton Farm** was once 'the new farmstead', that is, newer than the original settlement. Similarly, **Nobold** is 'the new building', although we must appreciate it was here by 1221. **Day House** comes from Middle English *dey*, which is used to speak of either 'dairy house' or 'dairy-maid's house'.

Many names end in the suffix 'gate' which invariably comes from Old English *geat* 'pass, entranceway'. However these names follow an element which informs us of what these places led to or from, which is not the case with the name of **Hookagate**. Clearly today a gate with a hook is as common as the field to which it leads, yet this is a comparatively recent development. Names are created to identify the place, thus will be as unique as possible. This name is quite possibly unique today, suggesting this is one of the earliest records of an actual gate as we would picture it.

# Merrington

The modern form has the element 'ing' which, if this is correct, suggests it follows a personal name. This is a prime example of how important it is to find as many early records of a place name as possible. Here the name is found from 1254 as *Muridon*, although the same place has a quite different entry in Domesday as *Gellidone* and similarly in 1245 as *Gulidon*. There is only one explanation for a place having two recorded names – once this must have been two very close places and, as they grew together to form one place, eventually became known by just one of these names.

*Merrington Well and the memorial to the Slaney family who paid for it to be sunk.*

The lost name seems to be an Old English name telling of 'Gelli's place at the hill'. However the modern name does not have a personal name but is from Old English *myrge* + *dun* which could be '(place at) the pleasant hill', or maybe this should be understood as 'hill where merry-making takes place'. Either definition is possible.

## Middleton Scriven

The basic name of Middleton is a common one, found throughout the country. With a little thought the name is probably easy to define. As it would seem from Domesday's record of *Middeltone,* this name means 'the middle farmstead' from Old English *middel* and *tun*. Although there is only one other example of this name in Shropshire, there are enough around the country to warrant a second distinguishing element. As with the majority this is a manorial reference, the Scriven family certainly had lands here by 1577 as evidenced by the record from that date as *Skrevensmyddleton*.

## Middleton Priors

This Middleton is unusual; it does not seem to have the same origin as the previous name and almost every other place in the country. Indeed the first element is uncertain. Listed as *Mittilton* in 1200 the suffix is undoubtedly from Old English *tun* 'farmstead' and, while the first element may well be *middel*, without further evidence it would be unwise to give this as the beginnings.

This is not the case with the addition; there are documented records of this place and surrounding lands being held by Wenlock Priory.

# Milson

There are records of this place from 1086 as *Mulstone* and from the thirteenth century as *Mulston* and *Muleston*. This name is thought to represent a Saxon personal name together with Old English *tun* giving 'Myndel's farmstead'. However this supposes that the modern form shows the possessive 's' and has become so slurred as to have lost an entire syllable over the centuries. Alternatives are hard to see, yet one may be Old English *myln* + *stan* meaning 'millstone'. It does not seem plausible that this is where millstones were cut, however it may be where they were brought to as a collection point, or perhaps this was where a rather unusual millstone could be seen.

# Minsterley

Domesday records this place as *Menistrelie*, while by 1246 it is found as *Munstreleg*. Undoubtedly this is from Old English *mynster* + *leah* which tells us this was the '(place at) the woodland clearing near or belonging to a minster church'. The most likely candidate is the minster church at Westbury.

The local here is the **Crown and Sceptre**, a place which has a name showing allegiance to the monarchy.

# Minton

Two records of note here, as *Munetune* in 1086 and *Muneton* in 1212. Although it may not seem it, this name is an indication of Shropshire's close proximity to Wales. Indeed the name is a hybrid of Welsh *mynydd* and Old English *tun* giving 'the farmstead near the mountain'. Of course the mountain in question is that now known as the Long Mynd.

*Fingerpost at Minton.*

# Monkhopton

The earliest record of this place is from 1255 as simply *Hopton*; however as this is of obvious Old English origin in *hop* + *tun* 'the farmstead in the valley', there is no doubt this name had existed long before the thirteenth century. Not until 1577 do we find the name closer to the modern version as *Munkehopton*. This addition refers to possession by the monks of Wenlock Priory.

Minor names at this place include **Cawley's Coppice** or 'calves woodland clearing'; **Skimblescott** which comes from 'Cenhelm's cottages'; **Sudford Dingle** or 'the horse ford'; **Quebb's Coppice** 'the marshy coppice'; **Wire Meadow** actually a weir on Beaconhill Brook; and **Hugger Moor** which features the dialect term 'hugger-mugger' speaking of 'a very wet or messy field'.

# Montford

A name which brings something of a picture of life in Saxon times, but also asks as many questions as it answers. With records as *Maneford* in 1086 and *Moneford* in 1255, this probably comes from Old English *gemana* + *ford* or 'the ford where people gather', the first element here is literally 'fellowship, association'.

Of course this tells of the gathering at the place on or near the ford, but does not tell us why they were gathering. However we would expect *moot* if this were a regular administrative gathering or *port* if it were a market. While there is no doubt the gathering would have been a regular one, we can also probably safely assume it was one of merriment.

Nearby **Preston Montford** has the very common addition which always refers to 'the farmstead of the priests', quite often a very complex way of stating this was land belonging to the church. Here is a field called **Quab Meadow**, the first part from Old English *cwabba* meaning 'marsh', and **Dinthill** which has only ever been found in this form and has completely baffled all who have tried to define it.

# More

Here we have an Old English element usually found in combination, although here it has somehow managed to remain on its own. This place is seen as *La Mora* in 1182, which is clearly based on Old English *mor* and telling us it was the '(place at) the marsh'.

# Moreton Corbet

Listed as *Moretone* in 1086, *Moorton* in 1334, *Mourton* in 1347, and *Moorton Corbett* in 1586. As with the following place this is the 'farmstead in a marsh'.

The addition refers to the Corbet family, who are found mentioned frequently from the thirteenth century onwards. Interesting to find the listing in 1271 as *Morton Turet* and in 1322 as *Morton Teret*, for this is the previous landholder of the Toret family. As the Torets had left the place by 1250 at the latest, it seems that their name lingered on in the place name for a generation or three afterwards.

*Moreton Corbet's once-proud castle.*

# Moreton Say

Whether this is found as Moreton or Morton the origins are the same – Old English *mor* + *tun* which could mean either 'farmstead in a marsh' or 'farmstead in moorland'. Indeed the name is so common it is often found with a distinguishing addition, as is the case with this place. Here the name refers to the manorial holding by the de Sai family, who are recorded here by 1199.

# Morville

Here is a name which sounds more as if it belongs on the North American continent than in Shropshire. However the suffix 'ville' is the result of a slurred pronunciation which has come to be reflected in the spelling. Recorded in Domesday as *Membrefelde*, as *Momerfeld* in 1200, as *Mainerfeld* in 1235, and *Momerefeld* in 1291, the suffix should be Old English *feld* meaning 'open land'. The first element is less certain, but is thought to be derived from something akin to Celtic *mamm* 'the breast-shaped hill'. Without clues which date from before Domesday it seems unlikely that this name will ever be defined with any certainty.

# Moston

This is usually only found as a minor place name and is always derived from Old English *mos* + *tun* or 'the farmstead in marshy land'. It seems likely the land used for farming would have been somewhat higher and therefore dry enough to be worked for at least the growing season.

# Munslow

With records such as *Mulslaye* in 1110, *Mulselawahundr* in 1187, *Munceloue* in 1261, and *Munsselawe* in 1256 it would normally be a simple task to define a name. However the first element is quite different in all these forms, which suggests the origin is not a well known one. The suffix is a different matter and is certainly from Old English *hlaw* 'mound or tumulus'. This *hlaw* normally follows an adjective or a personal name. The former seems unlikely as there are only a certain number of possibilities, thus this is almost certainly a personal name which has (so far) remained a mystery.

The field name of **All Rudge** comes from the description of a 'clay field with cultivation ridges' which must have been difficult to plough. **Broadstonel** is 'the broad stone' and refers to a bare rock revealed by soil erosion on Corve Dale. **Little London** is a name of a kind often found to refer to squatter's settlement, although it should not be taken as evidence that the people were from the place named. **Thonglands** is not what it seems but comes from Old English *tang land* and should be understood as a reference to the shape of this particularly 'narrow spit of land'.

At Munslow the **Crown Country Inn** has united two elements found in pub names in an effort to attract custom. The two halves show first allegiance to the monarchy and to the country, while the addition suggests a rural location and its traditional welcoming atmosphere and possibly a meal.

# Myddle

This Old English element is quite a common place name, usually found in combination. It does not mean 'middle' as it seems, but comes from *gemythel* and is recorded as *Mulleht* in 1086 and *Muthla* in 1121. This refers to the '(place at) the confluence of streams', which could be seen to be 'middle' in the sense of 'between the streams'.

The local has the most common pub name in the country, the **Red Lion**. As with all coloured animals the name is heraldic, the only remaining problem being to ascertain whose symbol. Clearly the number of pubs, at least six hundred at one time, must point to a major figure and there are two possible answers; this is either representative of John of Gaunt or possibly Scotland. Just which is impossible to say.

# Myndtown

Recorded in 1086 as *Munete*, in 1166 as *Muneta*, and in 1181 as *la Munede* this shows Shropshire's border with Wales and (as with Minton) the first element is from Welsh *mynydd* or 'mountain'. This must have remained to be '(place at) the mountain' for some time, indeed not until 1577 do we find a record closer to the modern form as *Myntowne*. While this is clearly an early 'town', it would be arguable if this place would be considered such today.

*The crests of the Long Mynd across the Shropshire countryside.*

# N

## Nash

What today seems more like a family name than a place name is actually both. However it is true to say that this would more commonly be found as a minor name. Records of this place are found as *Eshse* in 1242 and *Assh* in 1308, the latter a big clue as to its origins. From its beginnings in Old English *aesc* there is a later Middle English addition of *atten* which together describe the 'place at the ash trees'. The initial 'N' comes from the two elements being put together.

## Neen

There are two places in Shropshire with this name, **Neen Savage** and **Neen Sollars**. Both take there name from the same source, that of the River Neen which is an ancient British or Celtic name of uncertain origin and meaning. Today this river is known as the Rea. Early records of this name are found as *Nene* in 1086, *Nena* in 1193, *Niene* in 1195, and *Nenesauvage* and *Nen Solers* in 1272.

While the basic name remains a mystery, the additions are manorial names. The two families are known to be the le Savage family, who were resident by the thirteenth century, and the de Solers, known to be here by the late twelfth century.

## Neenton

As with the previous entry, this name has a first element from the River Neen which is today known as the Rae. Listed as *Newentone* in 1086 and *Nenton* in 1242, it does seem if the first element has been misunderstood by the Saxons and thought to be *niwe* as in 'new'. However this is certainly an Old English *tun* suffix and should be regarded as 'the farmstead on the River Neen'.

# Ness

An element more often found as a suffix, indeed the early records show the two places with this name recorded as *Nesse* and *Nessham*. This name is clearly from Old English *naess* telling us of '(the place at) the promontory or headland'. Both **Great Ness** and **Little Ness** are in a location which fit the name perfectly.

With the two little more than half a mile apart, it seems probable that there was once just one settlement, that most likely being at Great Ness and listed in Domesday as *Nessham,* 'the homestead at the promontory'. However there is no reason why Little Ness could not be the original, or just as easily fit the bill as being where the 'homestead' was erected.

There is also a **Nesscliffe**, a name of obvious origins, and better known for the cave here. **Kynaston Cave** was named after its most famous inhabitant, Sir Humphrey Kynaston. Born in 1474 he first came to prominence at the Battle of Blore Heath, a major confrontation in the Wars of the Roses. He ran into money problems while in residence at Myddle Castle and in 1491 was convicted of murdering John Heughes. Now an outlaw he took refuge in the cave, where he occupied one room and stabled his horse, Beelzebub, in the other. Here he embarked on a career as a highwayman, often described as a Salopian Robin Hood for his generosity to the poor and his targeting of the affluent. Eventually he received a royal pardon and moved to France where he died in 1534. Several legends may make his life sound a little unbelievable, yet the cave does exist.

# Newcastle

Of the three places with this name, Shropshire's must be the least known; it is the smallest and is certainly the most recent. Indeed, the first record found is from 1284 as *Novum Castrum* and means exactly what is says, it is '(the place at) the new castle'.

# New Invention

A very unusual name and, quite improbably, one of two in the Midlands. Even more astounding is that both are thought to have different origins. Both are comparatively recent, not being seen before the seventeenth century, and that is our biggest clue.

*This metal sheep at New Invention is not what the name refers to.*

Coinciding with the earliest days of the Industrial Revolution the name of the district of Wolverhampton is thought to have been derived from an oddball machine used in mining clay. Conversely the name of the Shropshire village most likely was once the name of the inn here. Of course it could be that both were 'named' at the same time, although the existence of the public house is required for this to work. Furthermore, the pub on its own is an acceptable idea. This is by no means the only place to have derived its name from a pub.

# Newport

It might seem an unsual place for a port. Even considering there are places which qualify as a port because of a navigable river, this place still has no chance of meeting the criteria. Hence there must be another reason, perhaps a misnomer. In fact it is our understanding of the modern use of 'port' which is misleading us. The original Old English *port* was used to mean 'market', and while a port can still be seen to be a market place the reverse was once the case.

Records of the modern form are found as early as 1237, while there is *Niweport* in 1050, *Nouus Burgus* in 1174, and *Neweburg* in 1232. Here is 'the new market town', which may suggest it was either deliberately founded to accommodate a market place in this region, or maybe the market was formerly held in another place, now lost.

Newport is the home to the only floodlit bike race in the land; started in 1970 it covers a circuit of 6 miles and was initially to promote the local business of Michael Jeggo and Doug Davies. Today it is known as the Newport Nocturne.

Streets here are named after an assortment of former residents. **Adams Close** recalls William Adams, a London haberdasher who was educated in Newport and who returned to found the Adams Grammar School with his newly acquired wealth. The Boughey family were also major benefactors in the town and are remembered by **Boughey Road**. **Powell Place** was built on the land where Powell's Waste Paper factory was demolished to make way for the development. **Tuckers Place** recalls the former Tucker's Ironmonger store.

The Audley family were lords of the manor for over two centuries from 1227 and justifiably deserve the naming of **Audley Road**. Sally Sandiford was a town councillor for many years and **Sandiford Crescent** was named to commemorate her work after she had left the position.

**Ben Jones Avenue** is named after the horseman, an Olympic medal-winner who was born in the town. Dr Elkington served as a GP to the town for many years, his work honoured by **Elkington Close**. Washerwoman Annie Snow was a long-term resident of the place now known as **Snow's Court**.

**Lapworth Way** is named after Lake Lapworth which, at the end of the last Ice Age, filled the depression in which Newport now sits. The names of **Lower Bar** and

**Upper Bar** were points leading into the town where, on market days, those heading in to trade were charged a toll for the privilege.

Locally is the **Barley Mow**, a pub name which shows the mow or stack of barley and indicates that beer was sold. The **Honeysuckle Inn** takes advantage of the pleasurable assault on at least two of the senses as an enticement, while telling what flowers were to be found there. Anyone who has experienced the heady scent of the honeysuckle in the evening would surely be tempted to sample this delicious aroma while enjoying a glass of their favourite tipple to unwind in the warmth of a summer evening. The **Pheasant** also takes advantage of a potentially attractive sign and a well-known sight in our countryside for its name.

The **Last Inn** proclaims itself the final drinking house in England before entering Wales. At one time licensing laws on either side of the border were very different and English holiday makers were often dismayed to find the pub closed on Sunday. It does seem a little short-sighted for surely when one is travelling in the opposite direction it would be the first inn.

# Norbury

A name found in several places throughout the land, always from Old English or Saxon *north* + *burh* or 'the northern stronghold'. Recorded as *Norbir* in 1237, it is not clear just what this place was north of or in relation to.

# Norton in Hales

There are many Nortons found throughout England, all of which are derived from Old English *north* + *tun* or 'the northern farmstead'. It is a matter of pure conjecture as to what this place was 'north' of; in order to say we would need to know exactly what was south of here at the moment this place was first known by this name.

Clearly the number of Nortons means a distinguishing addition is almost obligatory. Here the name refers to the name of the district of *Hales*, which is still in evidence in neighbouring Staffordshire, and comes from a plural form of Old English *halh* meaning 'nooks of land'.

The local is the **Hinds Head**, a break from the many Stag names and representative of the female deer. It still suggests a hunting area or someone associated with such, while also offering a different name.

# O

## Oakengates

This is a fairly recent name, or perhaps only more recent records have been traced, for we first find this as *Okenyate* in 1414. This comes from Old English or Saxon *acen* + *geat* which tells us it was '(the place at) the gate or gap where oak trees grow'. We should not expect this to refer to a gate as we would know it. Indeed, this refers just to an entrance or a way through. It is tempting to image it as a way to a field, as we would see in present times; however it is just as likely to be a way to a forest, a ford or even the sea.

Here we find a wealth of local names of interest. **Albion Street** was named from the **Albion Inn**, itself an early name for England. **Market Street** was the site of the market from the nineteenth century. There is a name found here as **Trench Farm** and **Trench Lodge**, which is actually found from 1306, earlier than that of Oakengates itself, as *apud Watlynggestrete et le Trenche iuxta Wimbrugge*. The Old French or Middle English *trenche* refers to a woodland road in a very special sense, which is with distinct clearings to either side, in effect giving a wider field of view and making it safer for travellers. Furthermore, there is an even earlier reference to this dated 1232 ordering the repair of several such places in Shropshire including this one. Thus this settlement is much older than the major place of today.

**Priorslee** is recorded as *La Leye* in 1255 and *Leg Prioris* in 1256, clearly a name from Old English *leah* with the lord of the manor being the Prior of Wombridge. Here is a name recorded as *Wombrugga* in 1186, *Wanbrege* in 1205, and as *Wanebrigg* in 1208, up to **Wombridge** of today. This is from Old English *wamb hrycg* or '(place at) the lake ridge'. Nearby is found **Hollinswood** which, although it may sound as if we should expect a personal name, does refer to the trees here – known to the Saxons as *holegn* this had plenty of holly. Lastly is **Snedshill**, recorded as *Snelleshulle* in 1271 and *Snead's Hill* in 1784, the earlier form is closer to the original 'Snell's hill'.

# Offa's Dyke

It would be difficult to explain this as a place name; the length of the feature makes it anything but a 'place'. This is a bank and ditch generally associated with Offa, the King of Mercia, constructed over a period of about forty years in the latter half of the eighth century. Listed as *Offedich* in 1184, the name of this defensive feature between England and Wales is self-explanatory.

The footpath which takes its name from this man-made feature runs for 177 miles from the Severn Estuary near Chepstow, to Prestatyn in the north. It follows a path passing many towns and castles, which blend with wetlands and mountains to produce a walk for all tastes. Shropshire's hills are probably the toughest leg of the journey, even for the most experienced walker.

Either side of the path is a region known as the **Marches**. The exact area defined as the Welsh Marches is indistinct, although historically it marks where skirmishes between the English and the Welsh were seen over much of the history of both peoples. Tradition would give it as the area between the mountains of Wales and the English river valleys, although today the term is applied to those counties which stand either side of the border.

The name is ultimately derived from the Proto-Indo-European word *mereg* which means 'edge' or 'boundary' although the same word also evolved to become the verb 'to march' in the sense of 'to patrol'. Obviously this is one of the earliest words in the language group.

# Oldbury

A reasonably common place name which is simple enough to define. Domesday lists this place as *Aldeberie*, which is further from the original Old English *eald* + *burh* than the modern form. Here we have 'the old fortified place', although just which other *burh* it is said to be old in comparison to is unknown.

# Onibury

An unusual name which requires a little creative thinking to define. Listed in 1086 as *Aneberie* and in 1247 as *Onebur* this seems to be 'the fortified place on the River Onny (or Onni)'. There is no record of this river name, although if it is correct it would come from two Old English words *ana* and *ea* referring to 'one' and 'river'. This place stands at the confluence of two streams and, if the river name is correct, would suggest a confluence.

# Oswestry

The five early records are of three distinctly different forms. Those of *Osewaldstreu* and *Oswaldestre* from 1190 and 1272 respectively undoubtedly show this to be '(place at) Oswald's tree'. Sandwiched between these is *Croesoswald* in 1254 which is a Welsh version meaning 'Oswald's cross' – Welsh influence should be expected owing to its close proximity. It should not be assumed that either the tree or the cross is incorrect, it is more likely that both existed and likely in the same place.

We also find the completely different *Blancmuster* from 1233 and *Blancmostre* from 1272. This certainly refers to 'the white minster' and, as two of these forms date from the same year of 1272, probably indicates a division between the two. Normally the separation would be a physical one; however, maps from around this time suggest otherwise. Hence the difference must have been either political or religious. Unfortunately no written record remains to show what the difference was. What is certain is that the division did not last much beyond the thirteenth century.

**Beatrice Street** is an old name, which makes suggestions of it being a personal name unlikely. It is thought to be a corruption of Middle English *badde* meaning 'poor, worthless' and suggesting it ran alongside or to land which was of poor quality.

**Denmark Place** was developed in 1864 and named to commemorate the marriage the previous year of Princess Alexandra of Denmark to the then Prince of Wales (later Edward VII). The hereditary Lords of Oswestry and Clun and Earls of Arundel are remembered in the name of **Fitzalan Road**. Similarly **Herbert Villas** were named after the Herbert family, Earls of Powys.

*Ivor Roberts-Jones, borderland farmer of Oswestry.*

*Oswestry's castle mound.*

Landowners Phillip Jennings and his family gave their name to **Jennings Road**, while **Warrington Place** similarly took the name of the Warrington Carew family. Less influential but likely more of an important individual as far as the public were concerned, Thomas Jackson is remembered by **Jacksons Yard**. The gentleman is recorded in the 1861 census as having a butcher's shop here.

The town walls were built in the thirteenth century and demolished four hundred years later. On the eastern side of the town the defence was correctly described as the **English Walls**. **Machine Yard** was the site of a public weighing machine from at least the 1860s, while **Pitcher Bank** recalls the somewhat over-zealous market traders yelling out their wares.

One of Oswestry's most famous sons gave his name to a part of the English language and, in the author's opinion, deserves to have a street named after him. 'The Lord is a shoving leopard' is one of the quotes attributed to William Archibald Spooner, who was attempting to say 'The Lord is a loving shepherd'. Such switching of syllables and letters between words have become known as Spoonerisms, much to the man's dismay during his lifetime.

Most inns said to be venues for cock fights are simply heraldic, it being unwise to advertise the practise after it was banned. It would seem from the addition of 'old' that the present name of the **Old Fighting Cocks** is a revival of an earlier name even though there is no documented evidence of a change of name.

The **Highwayman** might conjure up an image of a romantic rogue as portrayed by countless Hollywood heroes, yet the pub occupies the spot where many felons were hanged, including a number of highwaymen.

The **Three Pigeons** is an unusual name, thought to be a reference to the landlord or customers being affiliated with the Haberdashers and Threadmakers, thus heraldic. However just why such birds would have been chosen to represent these trades has always been a mystery.

Sometimes we find local history written on the signs of public houses. During the thirteenth century, Oswestry had a town wall known as the Black Gate, which stood until 1770. Today there is a record of this wall in the pub which is known as the **Black Gate**. The **Kings Head** shows the very recognisable image of Henry VIII, not that he had any connection with the pub but is simply used because he is still known five centuries later. The **Five Bells Inn** is a name which tells us instantly it has close connections with the church, the number of bells being what would have been in the tower when the pub was so named.

Some pubs have names referring to the products they hope you will buy, so it seems rather odd to have a place named **Last Orders**. This is the traditional cry which goes up before closing time, however this is not what is being suggested, that connection is solely to attract the attention of potential customers. The real reason for the name is answered by the location near the border with Wales; it suggests this is where one can get their last drink before leaving England.

# P

## Petton

As stated in the introduction, Domesday can be unreliable at times and its listing of this place as *Pectone* may seem erroneous at first. However we also have a record as *Pecton* from 1155, so it seems likely that this element is reproduced correctly. Therefore the only possible origin is Old English *peac + tun* which speaks of 'the farmstead by the pointed hill'.

While the nearest hill of any reasonable stature is over 2 miles away, it would still have been visible from here. Indeed, as place names are invariably given by neighbouring settlements (to residents it is simply 'home') the name was probably given by those who saw the hill beyond the farmstead.

This also explains the idea of a 'peak' when there are no peaks as we would understand them. Our idea of a peak is a high pointed snow-capped mountain; however this concept depends upon one's viewpoint. From a distance the view of a hill can be very different to those who are at its base.

## Picklescott

This name is very similar to the earliest forms available. Indeed these forms are very recent in comparison to most records, with *Pikelescote* and *Piclescot* being from 1231 and 1255 respectively.

It has been suggested that this comes from Old English *picel* meaning 'pointed hill'. However the suffix of *cot* is virtually unheard of to follow a topographical element, indeed it is normal to find it with a personal name. Thus the most likely definition is 'Picel's cottage(s)'.

# Pitchford

The number of early records for this name is more than adequate to define this origin. Listings include *Piceforde* 1086, *Picheford* 1194, *Pichford* 1176, and *Picford* 1242, all of which point to the Old English *pic* + *ford*. The name tells of '(place at) the ford near where pitch is found' and refers to the bitumen well near the crossing of the Row Brook.

# Plaish

This does not sound like a place name. Indeed, the Norman officers when surveying the land to prepare what was to become Domesday must have felt the same for they recorded the place as *Plesham*. This is not surprising, for the modern spelling is the exact pronunciation of the original Saxon or Old English word *plaesc* used to describe this region and which mirrors the record from 963 as *Plaesc*. This does not refer to the settlement itself but the region, for this is 'the shallow pool' and is also used to describe any region with still and shallow water. A clearly related word is found in another branch of the Germanic languages; from Middle Dutch comes *plasch*.

# Plealey

Found as *Pleyle* in 1256 and as *Pleyleye* in 1308, this name is clearly from Old English *plega* + *leah* and, even though the dates of these records would suggest otherwise, shows this place was known in the Saxon era. Indeed we can understand yet more about the origins of this place simply by defining the name.

This has its origins in 'sport or play in the woodland clearing'. If we look at this as originally being the Saxon equivalent of a sports ground which was later settled and the place took on the existing name, the evolution and the reason for the comparatively late appearance of the place is clear.

Sometimes defining a name can provide a glimpse into the lives of the Saxons and lets us see how the place would have looked with no painting or photograph to fall back on. Plealey is one such place.

# Plowden

A name which may seem very different from the previous listing of Plealey but is very similar indeed. This place is also first listed in the thirteenth century, as

*Plaueden* in 1252, but as with Plealey has had the name for much longer than this. Plowden comes from Old English *plaga + denu* and speaks of 'sport or play in the valley'. Here the origin is a slightly different word, although there are three Saxon words, *plaga*, *plaega*, and *plega*, which can mean 'play, sport, and game' and are interchangeable depending upon the context and/or tense in use.

# Pontesbury

This name is recorded in Domesday as *Pantesberie*, in 1203 as *Pantesbury*, in 1236 as *Pontesbiri*, and in 1242 as *Pantebur*. From these we can see there is no doubt the suffix is Old English *burh*. However the first element, which is certainly a personal name, seems to have two potential vowels. Indeed the correct definition is 'the fortified place of a man called Pant'. There is no personal name known as Pont, although today's residents must be grateful for the change in the vowel.

The school here is named after the author Mary Webb (1881–1927). She penned *Precious Bane, Gone to Earth,* and *Golden Arrow*, the latter inspired by the local story of a hidden gold treasure. The precious metal was fashioned into an arrow which was hidden somewhere on Earls Hill, a ritual hunt is conducted every Palm Sunday.

Pontesbury has a long history in mining, supplying local industries with coal, iron, lead and even stone. Its church has been here since the middle of the thirteenth century, was restored in the nineteenth, and is dedicated to St George.

**The Nags Head** is a pub name dating back to the days when a traveller could hire a pony or small horse to help with the journey. For those who feel the term 'nag' is an offensive description applied to some women, they might be interested to learn the term was only ever masculine until comparatively recent times.

*Pontesbury Hill, Shropshire.*

# Posenhall

Derived from Old English and listed exactly as the modern form as early as 1226. It tells us this settlement was built on a region which had already been described as 'a bag-shaped hollow of land'.

Locally **Bay Brook** is a name unknown until the modern maps of the twentieth century, thus is probably a local name which has been in use for generations. Officially it was recorded as *The Chesebroke* from at least 1454, which takes its name from *cese* and refers to 'cheese'. This would suggest this was once a thriving dairy farming community, but does not solve the mystery of the name change or where the new name for the brook comes from.

# Poynton Green

Listed in 1086 and 1255 as *Peventone* and *Pevinton* respectively, this is another name where a Saxon personal name is followed by Old English *tun*. This is a name which comes from 'the farmstead of a man called Peofa'. The addition of 'Green' seems to be an unwitting one, probably only originally applied to a village green. While it is true that there is a second Poynton, this is in Cheshire and over 50 miles distant so the addition is not for distinction.

# Preen

Actually this is the name of two places which are so close together as to be almost indistinguishable. The basic name is from Old English *preon* meaning 'brooch, pin'. Here the term is used to describe some feature in the landscape, most likely the hill upon which these places sit.

There are additions which distinguish the two names; **Church Preen** has its 'place of worship', **Holt Preen** is next to the 'wood'.

# Prees

Here is another name which shows Shropshire's close proximity to Wales, although the place is actually to the extreme east of the county about as far from the Welsh border as it is possible to get within the county boundary. This does not stop the name being derived from Old Welsh *pres* and describing '(the place by) the brushwood or thicket'. Early records of this name appear in the original Old Welsh in Domesday's *Pres*, and the first modern form of *Prees* in 1291.

# Presthope

The earliest listing of this name is from 1167 and is exactly as the current spelling of the name. However it is clear that this comes from Old English *preost + hop* and is 'the valley of the priests'.

# Preston Gubbals

As a place name Preston is one of the most common in the land. This is not surprising considering this means 'the farmstead of the priests', and that the church was second only to the monarchy as the most powerful landholders in England.

So common is this name that an addition is almost inevitable, especially for the smaller settlements. Domesday records this place as simply *Prestone*, the addition is not seen until 1292 as *Preston Gobald*. Unusually this is not a family name but that of the priest *Godebold*, who is recorded as landholder in Domesday.

Minor names here include **Bomere Farm** and **Bomere Heath**, the basic name telling us of 'the bull pond' and likely where such an animal was watered. **Pim Hill** is an odd name which has never been defined with any certainty but is normally given as 'the pimple-shaped hill'. The name of **War Hill** may seem clear, but there was no battle here; it actually comes from Old English *weard*, meaning 'watch or look-out hill'.

# Preston upon the Weald Moors

An Old English or Saxon place name from *preost tun* or 'the farmstead of the priests', referring to it being held by the church. The addition, as seen under Eyton upon the Weald Moors, is 'the wild moorland'.

Here we find local names such as **Kinley Farm**, from Old English *cyne leah* 'the royal woodland clearing'. There is no actual record of a royal holding, so this may be either a personal name or a reference to a hunting area. **Esp Spring** is something of a misnomer for there is no water here; this is a major corruption of the original Saxon telling us of the 'aspen copse'.

There is also the strangely named **Preston Argue Plantation**. The first and last elements do not require any explanation, yet the middle word seems completely unrelated. Indeed this element has proven difficult to tie down. If this place was nearer to the Welsh border it would be easy to see as coming from Welsh *argae* meaning 'dam' and telling us of irrigation channels here. This may well be the origin, especially considering there is no obvious alternative. It seems its location 30 miles east of Wales is the only thing stopping this being accepted.

# Pulley

This name has baffled all who have attempted to define it, even though there are three such names in the county. Listed as *Polelie* in 1086, *Polileg* in 1249, *Pillid* in 1304, and *Puleley* in 1321, there can be no doubt the suffix is from Saxon *leah* meaning 'woodland clearing'. For those who have some knowledge of how place names evolve, we should expect to find the first element from *pulig* or similar. However no word close to this is known, yet there must surely be a word for it is also seen in Pulley Vetus, in Meole Brace and Pully Foreign in Shrewsbury, both recorded in the tax record dating from 1763.

# Pulverbatch

There are actually two places here, **Church Pulverbatch** and **Castle Pulverbatch**, which are separated by less than half a mile and have additions which are self-explanatory.

It is the basic name of Pulverbatch which is the most intriguing. With records such as *Polrebec* 1086, *Piluerbach* 1262, and *Chyrche Pulrebach* in 1272, the suffix is from Old English *baece* meaning 'stream valley'. The first element is by no means certain but is possibly the name of the stream. If this is the case it is related to Norwegian *puldra* 'to gush', Swedish *porla* 'to purl' (the sound made by rippling water), and a number of similar words alluding to rapidly running water. Indeed, there is a dialect word *prill* meaning 'a rill', the beginnings of a channel cut by running water and is typically not only narrow but shallow, which was earlier seen as *pirle* and *purle*. It is this which is the most likely candidate for the stream name.

# Purslow

With records of *Posselaw* in 1086 and *Pusselawe* in 1226 we can see this comes from a Saxon personal name followed by Old English *hlaw*. The modern form has the 'r' which is a very late addition and can be put down to local pronunciation, for this is 'the tumulus of a man called Pussa'.

# Q

## Quatford

This name is unusual and the subject of much speculation. There are a number of forms found, although none are as telling as that from 896 as *Cwatbrycg*. Obviously there was also a bridge here at one time, a footbridge undoubtedly. This and other records would suggest a personal name, even though none of the listings show a possessive 's'.

We must also consider the following entry of Quatt, listed in Domesday as *Quatone* with the suffix *tun* meaning 'farmstead'. The two places are not that close to share a personal name, the name would have to be shared as it is too uncommon to be two different individuals, being almost 3 miles apart.

Thus this name most likely referred to a district known as *Cwat*. Indeed so unusual is this name it seems likely it was a nickname, although the meaning is completely unknown.

The local here has the unusual name of **The Danery**. The name is an error, based on an error, which explains why it is so odd. Old maps show the region where the pub was built to be known as the **Dennary**, whether the cartographer misunderstood the pronunciation or may simply have been incompetent, the region should have been the Deanery or, to give it its full name, the Deanery of the Collegiate Church of St Mary Magdalene.

## Quatt

See Quatford above.

# R

## Ratlinghope

Here is a name listed in Domesday as *Rotelingehope* and in 1255 as *Rotelinghop*. This features a Saxon personal name followed by Old English *inga* + *tun* giving us '(the place in) the valley of the family or followers of Rotel'.

The **Horseshoes Hotel** takes its name from the days when the inn was everything the garage mechanic is today, while the hospitality was undeniably superior. The horseshoe is easily recognised and would have been easy to attach to a wooden sign to show there was a blacksmith alongside for any necessary repairs.

## Roden

A very small hamlet has taken the name of the river, a lengthy tributary of the Severn noted for its wildlife. This is a Celtic or British river name meaning 'swift river' and is related to the Welsh *rhuthr* 'rush, attack', also British *rutuna* and even Latin *ruo*.

## Rodington

Early records as *Rodintone* in the eleventh century show this name comes from 'the farmstead on the River Roden' (see previous entry). The element 'ing' usually follows a personal name. However, here the familiarity with such names has meant this is expected and has crept into the spelling and pronunciation.

## Romsley

Recorded as *Hremesleage* in 1002, *Rameslege* in 1086, *Rameslea* in 1167, *Ramesleye* in 1212 and as *Rommesleye* in 1287, there is no shortage of available listings in order to define this name. Here Old English provides us with *hremn* + *leah* or '(the place at) the woodland clearing frequented by ravens'.

# Rorrington

Unlike the similar Rodington, the element 'ing' does follow a personal name. With records of *Roritune* 1086 and *Roriton* 1316, this is 'the farmstead of the family or followers of Hror'. Here Old English *inga* + *tun* follows a personal name which, although it appears Scandinavian, is Saxon and a nickname for someone known for being 'vigorous or strong'.

# Roughton

There are three places named Roughton, however the other two in Lincolnshire and Norfolk have different origins. Here records of *Rowton* and as the modern form in the early fourteenth century show this to be from Old English *ruh* + *tun* and is, somewhat predictably, 'the farmstead on rough ground'.

# Rowton

A name found in Domesday as *Routone*, in 1195 as *Rowelton*, in 1212 as *Ruelton*, and in 1233 as *Roulton*. While this is clearly an Old English or Saxon name, there are two possible origins. Either this is from *ruh* + *hyll* + *tun* and is '(the place at) the farmstead by a rough hill', or alternatively *ruhel* + *hyll* + *tun* 'the farmstead at the small rough place by the hill'.

# Rudge

An unusual place name in that it only has one element. Here the Old English *hrycg* is found alone, while it is normally found as a suffix. Recorded in Domesday as *Rigge* and as *Rugge* in 1188, the name tells us this was '(the place at) the ridge'.

# Rushbury

Three early forms of this name help us to define this name, as *Riseberie* in 1086, *Rissiberia* in 1180 and as *Russhebur* in 1283. Here the Old English elements *rysc* + *burh* combine to tell us of '(the place at) the brook where rushes grow'.

While the minor name of **Eastwell** would be difficult to see as anything other than 'the east spring', it must be considered uncertain for today there is no water course. **Lakehouse**, from *lacu*, should be considered to mean 'small stream' here unless the 'drainage ditch' was constructed for the original homestead in Saxon times. **Lushcott** takes its name from 'the cottage by the reeds', **Gretton** is 'the gravel settlement', **Stoneacton** was 'the stony oak farmstead', and **Millions Meadow** is something of an exaggeration for it was simply the site of the former mill. **Ape Dale** has never seen a simian, it actually refers to 'apple dale'; and **Crab Wood** is nothing to do with crustaceans but, once again, apples. **Wilderhope** was originally 'Withryd's remote valley', while it can still be see that **Stanway** was alongside 'the stone way'.

Someone clearly uncovered a valuable find at **Roman Bank** in early times, possibly coins but may also have been pottery or trinkets. However the most interesting name here must surely be **Spinny Bridge**, which comes from *spann* literally a 'span' or the breadth of a man's hand. As it refers specifically to the bridge we can deduce it referred to the width and thus must have been a footbridge. Here the name is used to convey what could well have been a tricky crossing.

# Ruyton-XI-Towns

It seems this is the only English name where Roman numerals are featured. This unique element is a very modern addition; the early forms simply give this as *Ruitone* in 1086 and *Ruton* in 1276. Derived from Old English *ryge* + *tun* this is 'the farmstead where rye grows'. The addition indicates this was once a parish composed of eleven townships or minor settlements.

# Ryton

A name which is of Old English derivation, from *ryge* and *tun* or 'the farmstead where rye grows'. Listed as *Ruitone* in Domesday is the village of Ryton, however there is also a **Great Ryton** to the east listed as *Ruiton* in 1209. This addition cannot really be for distinction with Ryton, the distance between them being almost 20 miles. We can only assume that Great Ryton was once two places and either the smaller is now lost or the two have merged as they grew.

*Ruyton-XI-Towns' central cross.*

# S

## Sambrook

Listed by Domesday in 1086 as *Semebre* and in 1285 as *Sambrok* this name was probably originally given to the water course here. From Old English *sand* + *broc* this is '(the place at) the sandy brook'.

The **Three Horseshoes Inn** is a name dating from the days when the horse was the only mode of transport. At this time the village blacksmith would be found alongside the inn, the metalworker offering a service to those who would make for the inn for refreshment. The number of shoes is relevant, a horse has four legs and a horse with only three good shoes would soon be lame. If the name is phrased as a question, then the place would have been the answer to the problem.

## Sandford

Even without the records of *Sanford* and *Sontford* from 1086 and 1236 respectively, it would not be difficult to understand the origins of this place name. Here the '(the place at) the sandy ford' returns its original Old English components of *sand* + *ford*.

## Selattyn

A very unusual sounding name, for two good reasons – the place has been influenced by its close proximity to Wales and Welsh, while the basis is a word seldom seen in place names. Records of this name are quite late as *Sulatun* and *Sulatton* in 1254 and 1420 respectively. This is from Old English *sulh* + *tun* which could refer to either 'settlement of the ploughlands' (extensive cropland) or 'settlement of the gullies' (irrigation channels). Clearly whatever the reason for the channels, they were prominent and seen annually for the name to have come about.

# Severn, River

The earliest known record of the name is as *Sabrina* in AD 115. Subsequently we find *Saeferne* in 757, *Habren* in about 800, *Saefern* in 896, *Hefren* in about 1150, *Sauerne* in Domesday, *Saverne* in 1140, and *Seuerne* in 1205. While we do know this is identical to an old stream name in Bedfordshire, and also has the same beginnings as the former name of the River Lee in Ireland (which was the Sabrann river), the meaning of this name is unknown. Obviously the sheer antiquity of the name does not help our investigation, yet it is a fairly safe assumption that it is has a different meaning to the usual 'flowing water' names.

*The Severn south from Ironbridge.*

# Shawbury

Domesday records this place as *Sawesberie*, with later records of *Shawberia* in 1165 and *Schagberia* in 1183. An Old English name from *sceaga* + *burh* and speaking of 'the stronghold by the small wood or copse'.

Just to the north of here is the small hamlet of **Acton Reynard**. This common place name is 'the farmstead by the oak trees'. It is easy to see why it is not unique, which is why a second distinguishing element is found – here a reminder that a certain Reyner de Acton was in residence by 1195.

The local at Shawbury is the **Elephant and Castle**. Since 1622 this has featured as the crest on the badge of the Cutlers' Company, the 'castle' is in fact the howdah on the back of the animal which then provided the ivory for the handles.

# Sheinton

This has been found listed as *Scentune* in 1086, *Seinton* in 1197, and *Shenton* in 1242 and is a place name which, depending upon how one interprets the early forms, can have two quite distinctly different meanings. That this name is of Old English derivation is certain, the problem here is the record from the end of the twelfth century, which may or may not show the existence of *inga*. If this element is present it would mean this place was 'the farmstead of the family of followers of Scena'. However without *inga* the personal name takes on the alternate meaning and the name becomes 'the beautiful farmstead' – the similarity with 'scenic' is clear.

# Shelton

Early records are not unlike that of the modern form as *Saltone* and *Shelfton*. This second form is particularly telling, for this is from Old English *scylf* + *tun* or 'the farmstead on the shelf of land or ridge'.

Here, too, is the region known as **Shelton Oak**, which means exactly what it says and requires no explanation. However it is recorded that in the 1950s a dead oak tree was removed in order for roadworks to be undertaken. If we needed any indication of the age of this notoriously slow-growing tree we only need to consult the record of a farmer from 1543, wherein he describes this same place as where there was an ancient tree, 'a grette oak'. There is also the local name of **Oxon**, which really is 'the hill of the oxen'.

# Shelve

Here is a place related to the previous name. Here the Old English is *scelf* and means exactly what it says, 'the shelf or land'. Early records of this place show it as *Schelfe* in 1180 and *Schylve* in 1249. This probably indicates this name was in existence before the settlement first appeared, as there is no mention of a home or farmstead.

# Sheriffhales

A name found in Domesday as simply *Halas*, yet by 1301 this had become *Shiruehales*. This basic name comes from Old English *halh* in a plural form meaning '(the place at) the nooks of land'. The other portion of this name is to give it some distinction, for *halh* is usually only found as a suffix. This is also Saxon, with *scirrefa* showing it was a possession of the Sheriff of Shropshire at the time of the Domesday survey.

*The sign at Sheriffhales is self-explanatory.*

# Shifnal

There are two records of note for this name, as *Shuffenhale* in 1315 and the remarkably early listing from 664 as *Scuffanhalch*. This is clearly an Old English *halh* following a Saxon personal name and speaks of '(place at) the nook of land of a man called Scuffa'.

A sixteenth-century coaching inn here was known as the Unicorn. However it is widely believed that Charles Dickens based many of the buildings in *The Old Curiosity Shop* on those he saw when he visited Shifnal. Hence the inn became known as **Nell's Place**, which was soon adopted as the official name and still is today.

The **Hare and Hounds** recalls the former bloodsport of hare coursing which was banned in 2002.

The **White Hart** is often said to be a hunting reference or possibly a heraldic representation, yet it was once used as a euphemism for any pub. Another typical pub name is that of the **Crown & Anchor**, which is derived from the badge of the Lord High Admiral and popular with former naval men who embarked on a new career as a pub landlord. That this sign is so common shows how the British Navy was the most powerful in the world for centuries.

The **Beehive** is a name which would have been representative of a place of work, where people were busy in an effort to provide a service and a sense of community.

# Shipley

A name found around England, also found as a minor name. Recorded in Domesday as *Sciplei* it has the same meaning as every other place of this name. Old English *sceap* + *leah* tells us this was '(place at) the clearing where sheep are grazed'. This also tells us something of the landscape even if we were unaware, for cattle are more profitable as livestock when the pasture is good enough to support them.

# Shipton

Listings have been found giving this name as *Scipetune* in 1086, *Sippton* in 1255, *Schipton* in 1256, *Parvum Scopton* in 1271, *Shupton* in 1360, and *Shepton* in 1607. While there is little doubt this is 'the farmstead where sheep are found', the name does show a 'Little Shipton' dating from 1271 which would suggest a second settlement. However no record of a *Magna Shipton* has been traced, which leads us to the conclusion this was a mistake on the behalf of the recorder.

Here we find the highly descriptive name of **Larden**, which can only come from Old English *laefer denu* and telling us of 'the valley where wild iris grows'. There is also the delightfully named **Mogg Forest**, which has two possible Middle English origins. This is either from *mug* and is 'muddy', although hopefully this comes from *mucg* giving us 'where mugwort grows'.

# Shrawardine

Here is a Saxon name derived from Old English *scraef + worthign*, as evidenced by records such as *Saleurdine* 1086, *Shrewardin* 1165, *Shrawurdin* 1166, and in 1212 *Srawurthin*. This name means 'enclosure near a hollow or hovel'. The greater likelihood is 'hollow', for the name is shared with **Shrawardine Pool** around half a mile north of the village and this is probably the hollow spoken of.

Doubtless the name once only applied to one of these places. It was the close association of the two which resulted in the name being shared.

# Shrewsbury

The county town has a number of early forms worthy of mention. In 901 *civitas Scrobbensis*, by 1006 *Scropesbyri*, ten years after that as *Scrobbesbyrig*, as *Sciropesberie* in 1086, and in 1094 as *Salopesberia*. This variety of forms points to a Saxon origin of *scrobb + burh* giving us 'the fortified place of the scrubland region'. Not a particularly flattering definition for what is a delightful place today. However there can be no doubt that this was the origin. The name was simply a description of the place; there was never any deliberate attempt to make this or any other place sound unattractive. In Saxon times Shrewsbury was found in an area of scrubland.

**Albrightlee** takes its name from its location in being 'the woodland clearing adjacent to Albrighton'. What is surprising is the ending has evolved as 'lee' and not the usual 'ley'. Around Albrightlee we find the name of **Featherbed Lane**, a common enough name always referring to an almost perpetually muddy surface. One interesting field name here is that of **Lion Coppice**, which actually takes its name from the Red Lion public house which stood here in the nineteenth century.

The street names in and around the administrative centre of the county range from the predictable to the unique. **Butcher Row** is a name of obvious meaning, yet while we might have also recognised the listing of 1580 of *The Flesh Boordes*, it seems unlikely that we would know the Shambles as it was once called. Here is a name from Middle English *sceamol* which went on to become a market stall for meat and meat products alone. **Fish Street** is another name of obvious derivation, so is **Milk Street** but as far as we know there is only one other and that it is in London.

**Castle Street** clearly takes its name from the town landmark, **Church Street** refers to St Alkmund's, yet while **Town Walls** is a name needing no explanation it is surprising to find it was not a street before 1871. However, while **Raven Meadows** certainly has its basis in the bird, it is a rather circuitous route from the landholders, to their coat of arms, to the **Raven Arms** pub which took the emblem for a name. Also here was the cattle market which gave rise to **Smithfield Road**, which has no etymological value in Shrewsbury but is simply a name 'borrowed' from London.

The Raven is not the only place to take its name from a pub. **Bear Steps** comes from the Bear Inn which stood in Fish Street until the early twentieth century. **Gullet Passage** may come from Middle English *golet* or Old French *goulet*, meaning 'a channelled stream, or gullet' and which is recorded here in 1696. However there is also an inn called the Gullet documented in 1526. It seems logical to suggest the water channel came first, yet there is no written proof. **Swan Hill** remembers the Swan Inn at the corner off **Cross Hill**, itself a road allowing pedestrians to cross between here and our next street name. **St John's Hill** comes from a time when the tailors and skinners guild dedicated their chantry in St Chad's Church to St John the Baptist.

People have also given their names to streets such as **Pride Hill**, which recalls the family of that name who were around here by the thirteenth century. The Windsor family owned **Windsor House** by 1799, a name which was transferred to **Windsor Square** and **Windsor Street**. **Beeches Lane** remembers local wool merchant Roger Beche, who was paying taxes here by 1580, while a century earlier **Carnarvon Lane** was the home of Ludovick Carnarvon. The Cole family gave their name to the house which later became the region known as **Colehall**. John Hill, who became mayor of Shrewsbury in 1689, gave his name to **Hills Lane**. Hill lived at **Rowley's House** which took its name from William Rowley, a seventeenth-century draper and brewer.

Home to William Beacall in 1800 it was to become known as **Beacall's Lane**. **The Dana** was named in honour of the Revd Edward Dana who busied himself with the creation of the riverside walk until his death in 1823. **Howard Street** recalls the life of prisoner reformer John Howard (1726–90), and **Nettles Lane** was the abode of John Nettells in 1623.

Not only people but their lifestyles in the form of trades and religions have made a mark. **Greyfriars Bridge** and **Greyfriars Road** recall the former Franciscan friary. Similarly **Priory Road** and **St Austin's Street** remember the Augustinian canons of that order. The parish of **Holy Cross** and **St Giles** takes the names from the church better known as Shrewsbury Abbey, and a twelfth-century leper hospital.

**Barker Street** takes its name from Middle English *barkere* meaning 'a tanner of leather'. **Bleaching Ground** is a field name telling us this was where flax was bleached. While the oldest profession of them all, or so we are told, is seen in **Grope Lane**. Indeed, early forms from the fourteenth and sixteenth centuries leave us in no doubt this was the red light district of its day. Even though we may consider 'grope' being used in a sexual sense as modern slang, this is exactly what was being said about this street almost a thousand years ago.

Until 1900 **English Bridge** was recorded on maps as Stone Bridge, referring to its construction. However in earlier times it was also known as Shropshire Bridge and Abbey Bridge. The modern name was doubtless influenced by the name of **Welsh Bridge**, a name in use from the sixteenth century replacing the earlier St George's Bridge, and probably an indication of where the labourers came from. Another major stone construction has given a name to **Castle Foregate** which, although it might seem to be obvious, is used to infer this place was 'outside the town walls'.

While we know the origins of **Wyle Cop**, understanding the meaning is a different matter. It should be seen that although we know a great deal about the Saxon tongue, it is impossible to know everything and may be difficult to interpret. This is particularly true of words with two (or more) meanings. This second element of the name certainly comes from the Old English *copp* 'hill summit', the first element is understood as 'contrivance'. This should probably be defined as 'invention' and, when combined with the second, may be telling us of winding gear used to raise goods up this very steep incline.

The name of **Bellstone** describes a 'bent or curved stone', specifically the large boulder which stood here until the 1930s. **Claremont Hill** is one of those names where the first part has been misunderstood, for the French *mont* means 'hill'. Together this name can be defined as 'the beautiful hill hill' which, although it may seem a little odd, is by no means unique.

While the name of **Mardol**, also found as **Mardol Quay**, is well documented over the centuries, there is no known origin which can be offered. Any suggestion it has been transferred from the same name found at Much Wenlock can be discounted, as the records from Shrewsbury are much earlier.

**Rowshill** is a minor name from '(the place at) Hror's hill'; this is also seen as Old English *hror* meaning 'strong, vigorous' and is thus probably a nickname. Old records show that the **Shoplatch** is a corruption of *Schoteplace*, a name meaning either 'the archery place' or 'open space in the town'. A map of the area around Austin Friary

*Shrewsbury's imposing abbey.*

reveals the field name of **The Mud Holes**, which speaks of the culvert which ended here. It brought the town's sewage which was later carted away as manure. It is also recorded as **The Spout Hole**, **The Sink Hole** and **The Muck Hole**.

**Ditherington** comes from a derogatory term, 'the shivering settlement', obviously once the abode of the exceptionally poor in this neighbourhood. **Factory Bridge** was built near to the linen factory which stood here from 1796. **Coleham** stands at the confluence of the Rea Brook and the Severn; the first element is possibly the personal name Cola suffixed by *hamm* taken here to mean 'with much water around'. The name of **Hermitage** is a transferred one, for the original was attached to St Mary Magdalene. Indeed it is recorded as being granted to Roger, a hermit of Shrewsbury, in 1356.

From a Saxon personal name followed by Old English *eg* comes 'Kent's raised ground in marsh', today known as **Kempsey**. Recorded as *cotes* in 1175, **Coton** is certainly plural and describes 'the cottages'. **Roundhill** is simply 'the rough hill', **Cadogan House** takes its name from a thirteenth-century cross, while **Frankwell** is an Old French name telling us it was 'the free town' and thus enjoyed special tax privileges.

**Harlescott** was listed as *Herlaveschote* in 1160 and *Erlauscote* in 1199. It comes from the Saxon personal name with an Old English *cot* meaning 'Herelaf's cottages'. Here is found a field name, **Scotchet's Leasow**, which was home to the Cotchet family by 1893. A similar name, with similar origins, is **Hencott** which is recorded as *Hennechothe* in 1160, *Henecot* in 1203, and *Ennecote* in 1208 and refers to 'the cottages where hens are reared'.

**Oldheath** is an obvious name. It meant exactly the same in Saxon times as it does today. Indeed it has changed little in hundreds of years. Likewise **Darville** can still be seen as being from *deor fald* or 'the deer enclosure'. Yet **Crosshill**, which does stand at a road junction, is unlikely to refer to a signpost as the forms are too early and thus probably does refer to a religious cross which once stood here. **Sutton** is a common name always referring to 'the southern farmstead' and also gave its name to the medicinal spring here in 1851 of **Sutton Spa**. Furthermore, the name of **Coalpit Cottages** is a reminder of a time when charcoal burners lived here.

**Cut Throat Lane** seems to have been the site of an attempted murder in 1801. Four soldiers robbed a farmer and left his bruised and bleeding body for dead. However the victim was made of stronger stuff and managed to crawl into the town. His description led to the arrest of the men at a pub in Castle Street and the lane acquired its gruesome name.

The region known as **Judith Butts** may seem to be simply a reference to a personal name, yet the record of 1508 shows this as *Judas Buttis* and thus is something else entirely. From Old English *butte* the last part refers to 'a small strip of land'. Judas is a common field name used to refer to either 'poor land' or perhaps 'the elder tree' which has always been associated with Judas Iscariot.

**Tankerville Street** is on land owned by the Earl of Tankerville, while between Rad Brook and the River Severn is **Kingsland**, a name which might seem of obvious origin yet there is no documented evidence to indicate this was 'the king's land'. Incidentally the name of the **Rad Brook** comes from the nearby **Redhill**, itself telling exactly what its origins are, while the water course has evolved to first *Raddle* and then shortened to *Rad*. Earlier it was known as the *Pintle Brook*, which comes from the name of a plant which grew here such as the cuckoo-pint or, in Middle English, *pintel*. Another plant gave its name to **Dogpole**, from Middle English *docce pol* this is probably 'dock pool' but could possibly be another plant, the water lily.

Many records in Shrewsbury speak of narrow passages. Known locally as 'shuts', the term has had several suggested definitions. The most likely meaning is the feeling of being 'shut in or enclosed', a reference to a thoroughfare so narrow it can only have been used by pedestrians.

There are numerous examples, such as **Bank Passage**, formerly known as *Twenty Steps Shut;* the later name comes from the bank which stood here until 1910. In 1812 **Castle Court** was known as *House of Correction Shut*, for that was what was there. **Seventy Steps Passage** had at least three other names in its history: *Burley's Shut*, the name of a painter at the lower end of this walkway in 1728; *Waggon and Horses Shut*, an inn which was reached via this walkway; and *Hundred Steps Shut*, which is an exaggeration, not a miscount!

**Drayton's Passage** took its name from the name of a nineteenth-century printer who had his premises here. During the previous century the same venue was the workplace of another printer, who also gave his name to *Eddowes Shut*. **Peacock Passage** from 1795 was previously *Kings Head Shut* in 1674, both referring to public houses which stood at opposite ends of the path. Mr Phoenix was a baker in the early twentieth century after whom **Phoenix Passage** was named; earlier family names had produced *Mason's Shut* and *Shackleton's Shut* for the same place.

Shrewsbury's pub names are taken from various sources, reflecting the history of the town as well as the trade. From the days when the horse was the only mode of transport come the names of the **Stables** and the **Coach and Horses**, which doubtless is also the more subtle reference in the name of **The Beaten Track**. The **Telegraph** is another which, despite the more obvious meaning of the signalled letter, is more

*A delightful Shrewsbury milepost.*

likely to honour the fastest stagecoach on English soil. Other more unusual and diverse modes of transport are marked by the **Steam Wagon Inn** and the **Coracle Inn**. The latter refers indirectly to the river, which is also the subject of the **Cygnets** although the young was chosen rather than the Swan for it described the re-birth of a pub formerly known as the Swan.

People are a popular source of names for pubs too. The **Harry Hotspur** remembers the eldest son of the 1st Earl of Northumberland who was renowned for his gallantry as much as his short temper. The **Prince of Wales** is a title conferred on the eldest son of the reigning monarch when he comes of age. Having been the case since the early fourteenth century, there are many it could refer to, although most commemorate one of the longest-serving, the eldest son of Queen Victoria and future Edward VII. The **Charles Darwin** is named after Shrewsbury's most famous son, the man who first published the theory of evolution. **The Admiral Benbow** is named after the naval officer who was born in Shrewsbury and was killed during a long battle with the French in the Caribbean.

Granted its coat of arms in 1473, the master builders and secret society would have met at places such as the **Masonic Arms**. The **Britannia** is a patriotic reference to the Roman name for Britain. The **Hop & Friar** is an unusual combination for a name; however it is simply a reference to the long association between the pub and the church and to suggest the monks were brewing their own ale as the water would have been a possible source of illness. The name of the **Romping Cat** is a popular nickname for a heraldic lion which has since been adopted as its official name, while the **Vaults** shows this has not always been a pub but was once used solely as a storehouse for wines and spirits.

**Albert** is a name which honours the consort of Queen Victoria, her beloved Francis Albert Augustus Charles Emmanuel, Prince of Saxe-Coburg-Gotha (1819–61). **Bellevue** is a name derived from the French for 'beautiful view' and is found when there is a pleasing vista to behold. The **Three Fishes** is a somewhat veiled religious reference, the fish being associated with St Peter and the number representative of the Holy Trinity.

Finally the name of the **Lloyds in the Town** was the site of a tyre depot which was redeveloped as the Victoria. Being supplied by the town brewery of Lloyds and Trancer, when Ansells took over the brewery the pub was renamed to remember one half of the original brewer.

# Shropshire

The name of the county is found in Domesday as *Sciropescire*. This is a shortened form of the old spelling of Shrewsbury together with Old English *scir* which is today written 'shire' and simply refers to an administrative 'district'.

For a few years towards the end of the twentieth century it was decided to change the name of the county to **Salop**. This change was not well received and the original name was soon reinstated. From an etymological point of view the alternative Salop has no different origin to Shropshire; it is only the shortened form of the name used by the Normans. Indeed the motto on the county council is *Floreat Salopia* or 'May Shropshire flourish' and the residents are still referred to as 'Salopians'.

*The sign says it all, Buildwas.*

# Shropshire Union Canal

In these days of high speed travel the names of the earlier routes are often misunderstood. The great route which was completed over two hundred years ago is an example of such. The canal system of the country was not constructed with a nationwide network in mind. Each section was built to serve a specific purpose and funded by the region's industry, much the same as the earliest railway lines. The 'Union' was of the companies who founded the Ellesmere Canal, the Birmingham & Liverpool, the Montgomeryshire and links the network in the Midlands with the River Mersey and the Manchester Ship Canal. The company formed to link the various segments also constructed railways through the county.

# Sibdon Carwood

For those who have read elsewhere in this book that a second element (such as that seen here in Sibdon Carwood), invariably comes from a manorial family may think this seems a good example. Indeed it seems that either of the halves may well refer to the family who were lords of this manor in early times. Yet this is a name which is entirely of Old English derivation; even the personal name is Saxon.

Listings of this name are found as *Sibetune* 1086, *Sibbetone* 1166, and not until 1672 is the modern name seen in *Sipton Carswood*. Clearly the place was simply Sibton for many years, the personal name being suffixed by *tun* as 'Sibba's farmstead'

– pronunciation and association with Old English *dun* has meant the evolution to the current form.

The second part is also found in early records, as *Carwod* in 1307. Doubtless this is from *carr* + *wudu* 'the wood where rocks are found'. Carwood is still shown on maps near the village.

# Sidbury

Domesday's *Sudberie* is followed by *Sudberi* in 1176, which leave the origins in no doubt. Here the Old English *suth* and *burh* combine to tell us this was 'the southern fortified place'. This suggests there was another *burh* to the north, the most likely candidate being Oldbury, south of Bridgnorth.

# Siefton

An unusual name which has two possible, and quite diverse, origins. Listings of this name are found as *Sireton* 1086, *Ciraton* 1086, *Siveton* 1257, and also *Syueton* in the thirteenth century. In fact the name has been found as Seifton on official documentation as recently as the late nineteenth century. Whether this can be considered to be evidence of uncertain spelling is debatable, more likely this is an administrative error which has gone unnoticed.

The most commonly quoted origin for the first element here is a Saxon female name and given as 'Sigegifu's farmstead'. However there is growing support for the alternative of the stream name *Siven*, which is clearly related to that of the better known Severn and (as discussed earlier in this book) has defied all attempted to explain it. The suffix is clearly the common Old English element *tun*.

# Snailbeach

This name is applied to a district, a farm, and a railway, while historically the name also referred to a mine. Since Roman times, lead has been mined here, right up until it was closed in 1955. Galena, the ore from which lead is smelted, was particularly rich here and it has been claimed to be the greatest volume lead-producing mine anywhere in Europe. Indeed, there are still thought to be vast quantities of the metal ore still to be removed from the lower reaches. However these are over 1,000ft underground and have been deemed unsafe to continue working. Smaller quantities of other minerals and metals are to be found here, including silver and zinc.

The village grew solely because of the mine, the narrow gauge railway built to link the workings to the main line at Pontesbury. As with the conserved mine buildings, it is planned to restore and re-open the railway as a preservation line for passenger traffic which can only serve to increase interest in the site.

Obviously the name of the place is nothing to do with either of these, nor is it a reference to the farm. In 1799 there is a record of *Sneilbach Mines* and in 1836 as *Snailbeach*. However, the name is much older and comes from either Old English *baece* 'stream valley' or Middle English *bache* of the same meaning. The first element is self-explanatory, the word having existed for centuries, which makes this 'the valley of the stream infested by snails'.

# Stanton Long

The basic name here comes from Old English *stan tun* 'the farmstead on stony ground'. The additional 'Long' is of obvious meaning and was not seen before the thirteenth century. However the settlement has always been closer to an exaggerated bone shape, with two larger clumps joined by a narrower portion.

Local names include **The Meers** or 'boundary fields', **Oxenbold** 'where oxen are housed', and **Patton** is 'Peatta's farmstead'. Another name here allows us a detailed glimpse into life in the Dark Ages. What appears to be an oddly named **Hill Oddy Leasowe** is in fact a corruption of Kiln Hoddy which we know refers specifically to 'a pit for drying flax'.

# Stanton upon Hine Heath

Clearly a name comprised of two quite separate elements, even before we consult the records of *Stantune* in Domesday and *Staunton super Hyne Heth* in 1327. The first part is common in place names and is invariably derived from Old English *stan + tun* 'the farmstead on stony ground', although it could sometimes be interpreted as 'the farmstead near standing stones'.

This addition is from the later Middle English *hine + hethe*, the name given to 'the heath of the household servants'. The suggestion here is that land was given over to the families of those working for the lords of this manor for their own use; although it should be assumed that a percentage of the produce was taken in rent.

The local inn has taken a rather unimaginative name in the place name as the **Stanton Arms**. While it may show local pride there must surely be local history to draw upon.

## Stanwardine

A name recorded as *Staurdine* in Domesday and in 1193 as *Stanwardin*. This is undoubtedly of Old English origin in *stan* + *worthign*, although whether this suggests 'the enclosure on stony ground', or an unusual but not impossible 'enclosure constructed of stones' is uncertain.

## Stapleton

A name found throughout England, often as a minor name. It is derived from Old English *stapol* + *tun* and describes the 'farmstead marked by a post'. This place is only found once in early records, as *Stepleton* in the thirteenth century.

## Stirchley

Quite early records of this name are found, as *Styrcleage* in 1002 and *Stirchelega* in 1167. This name is of Old English derivation in *styrc* + *leah* and speaks of 'the clearing for young bullocks'.

This is one of those names which reveals more than would first seem. We are told that cattle are raised, meaning it must have been a place where the pasture was of good quality. Furthermore this farming must have continued for a reasonable length of time in order for the place to acquire the name, from which we can deduce that these farmers were excellent at raising livestock for its beef.

Locally are **Holmer Cottage**, **Holmer Farm** and **Holmer House**, with the basic name from Old English *ule mor* 'the marsh frequented by owls'. **Randley Brick Works** takes its name from **Randley Wood**; the name here is from *rand leah* or 'the woodland glade at the border'. Another two places sharing a name are **Lower Brands** and **Upper Brands**, a 'brand' being a place which has been cleared by burning.

## Stokesay

A name recorded as *Stoches* in 1086 and as *Stoksay* in 1256. It features the common element *stoc*, the Old English term used here to speak of 'the outlying (possibly seasonal) farmstead'. The second element here is actually a manorial name, from the family of de Say who were here in the twelfth century. Normally this would have evolved as two names, were it not for the fact that there are only two syllables and they run together so readily.

*Two views of Stokesay Castle.*

Stokesay Castle is in fact a fortified manor house. Completed in 1291, it is one of the best preserved examples of its kind and has hardly altered in eight centuries. The view from the top of the tower has changed little since the author Henry James stayed here in 1877; only the glimpse of a passing car or electricity pylon reveals modern life.

# Stoke St Millborough

A common basic name from *stoc*, here used to describe a 'dependant settlement'. The addition comes from the well here, **St Milburgha's Well**. First recorded in 1321 it was said to be capable of miraculous cures, indeed it became a place of pilgrimage. Milburga was an abbess of Wenlock Priory and a daughter of a King of Mercia. Various stories are told about her, including a remarkable power over birds and the ability to levitate.

There are numerous local names of interest. **Gibbridge** refers to the 'ridge with a hump'; **Ripletts** is a 'strip of land'; **Bockleton** was originally 'Boccel's farmstead'; and **Kinson** was 'Cynestan's farmstead'. **Cleedowntown** has the predictable definition of 'the farmstead on the lower slopes of Clee Hills' and is clearly related to **Cleestanton**, 'the stony farmstead on Clee Hills'. **The Toot** means 'look out place' and is at the point where several well-worn tracks come together on Brown Clee.

**The Friths** is very English name describing 'scrubland', **Dumble Hole** is from *dumbel* 'the hollow overgrown with trees'. **Dial Yard Meadow** is a minor name found throughout England and always referring to 'the place with sundials', although this is often the only remaining indication that such existed here. **Pel Beggar** is a farm on the southern boundary which may well have got its name from a single incident where 'a beggar was repelled'.

However the most interesting name here is that of **Scirmidge**, noted as *The Skirmish* in 1784. As can be seen from the eighteenth-century record, it was a place of conflict. Indeed it was not for many years that this 'disorderly place' became part of this or any other parish, for that is what is indicated here. Yet this island between the parishes was to come in useful. It seems that a cottage here was home to a midwife and, between 1784 and 1796, three neighbouring parishes sent every unmarried pregnant woman within their boundaries to this place. Now their consciences were clear – the best healthcare available for mother and child, while the parish no longer had the problem to deal with. During this short period no less than fifty-two illegitimate births are recorded at this one cottage.

# Stottesdon

Both Domesday's *Stodesdone* and from 1160 the record of *Stottesdun* show this is an Old English name derived from *stod + dun*. Here two elements combine to give a glimpse into the early days of this village, which was where 'a herd of horses were kept'. The element *stod* is also used to refer to a 'stud' in the modern sense. While there is every chance this was what was happening, there are insufficient records available to confirm this to any degree of certainty.

# Strefford

This is found as *Streford* in 1255, but it is the earlier Domesday record of *Straford* which is of more interest. Knowing the meaning of this name, we would expect it to have evolved to something more akin to Stratford, which is the most common form of this Old English *straet + ford*. Here is a derivation found all over England as the '(place at) the ford on the Roman road'.

# T

## Tasley

An unusual name which has proved difficult to define. Recorded in 1230 as *Tasselegh* and three years later as *Thasseleg*, these examples are rather late and rather too close together along the timeline to give any clues. Doubtless the suffix is Old English *leah* 'a woodland clearing'. However this suffix does not particularly favour any first element, being found in combination with personal names, fauna, flora and numerous adjectives. It is tempting to suggest a personal name but none readily come to the fore.

## Telford

A very modern name indeed, commemorating the work of the engineer Thomas Telford (1757–1834) and whose work can still be seen. Even if you have never heard of the man and never seen the town you will doubtless have seen something of his work. His legacy is all around in the form of bridges, roads, and the canals. Even the streets recall the history of the place, such as **Ironmasters Way**, **Colliers Way**, **Boulton Grange**, **Brunel Road** and **Forge Gate**.

A district of Telford which was named long before the engineer was even born is **Malins Lee**. The name is recorded as *Malineleg* 1261, *Leygh Malin* 1292, *Maleyneslegh* 1301, *Malinsly* 1630, and *Malins Lee* 1736 and provides a problem for those trying to define the name. The most likely explanation is that this is actually one word, where a Middle English female name has been suffixed by *leah* giving 'the woodland clearing associated with a woman called Malin'.

Here are found **Abbey Villas** adjoining the ruined chapel, **Stone Row** erected by coal and iron workers in the early ninth century, and **Spout House** from Middle English *spoute* which means what is says, used in the sense of 'gutter, water pipe'.

The most important items on any pub's agenda are the customers. Without members of the public calling in for a glass or two of their favourite tipple the business will not last long. Hence from the earliest days pub names were created to invite potential customers inside, particularly important when most of the custom was passing trade and hence the name of the **Travellers Joy**. Similarly the original **All Labour In Vain** was a remark designed to convey that, no matter how hard anyone tries to produce an ale as good as that found within they will 'all labour in vain'.

Telford's connection with the railways is marked by one of the world's most famous locomotives in **The Mallard**, a popular choice for a pub name associated with the railway. There is a **Wren's Nest** here, a name found only in the Midlands and which became more popular after the demise of the old farthing coin – Britain's smallest bird was featured on the reverse. However, here the name is taken from **Wrens Nest Lane** which seems to have been a long time abode of the species.

The **Blue Pig** is a name which shows Telford's industrial heritage. When the molten iron flows on smelting, it travelled down conduits to pits where it solidified turning a distinct shade of blue. The way the small troughs were lined up along side the furnace reminded the workers of piglets suckling their mother and thus the fresh casting was referred to as a 'blue pig'. The **Bulls Head** probably started life as a religious sign, a reference to the seal of the papal bull. The **Bell and Bails** was previously known as the Quarry Inn, where the stone was cut to build the church which is one side of the inn and gives the 'Bell' part of the name. On the other side of the inn is the local cricket ground, which provides the 'Bails'.

*A sculpture erected in 1993 to mark twenty-five years of Telford in its popular parkland.*

# Teme, River

A British river name related to names such as Tene, Tame and Tamar, or Welsh Taff, the base word now lost but certainly related to Old Irish *temen* and even Sanskrit *tamas*. Along with the vast majority of names given to watercourses which have come down from before Roman times it is highly simplistic and refers to 'the dark one'.

To have a name which is related to such ancient tongues with the Indo-European group shows just how long this name has been in existence. It is a sobering thought to consider this name may well have been in use almost from the time when the ice sheet receded from the land and the first waters of the Teme flowed through Shropshire.

# Tern, River

A Celtic river related to the Welsh *tren* and meaning quite literally 'the strong one'. Even today the current is noticeably swift, at least two thousand years after the name was first used.

# Tibberton

A name also found in Worcestershire and Gloucestershire. These are unrelated except in that they share identical origins in a Saxon personal name with Old English *tun*, although it should be understood this was simply a common name and not the same individual. Recorded as *Tetbristone* in Domesday this is 'Tidbeorht's farmstead'.

# Tilstock

Shropshire may well be able to claim more places featuring female personal names than any other county in England, for this is another example. First recorded in 1211 as *Tildestok* this is 'Tidhild's specialised place'.

# Tong

Between 1002 and 1317 this place is recorded as *Twongan, Tvange, Twanga, Tange* and *Tweongan*. Along with a similarly named place in West Yorkshire, this is thought to be Old English *tang* which refers to 'the feature shaped liked tongs'. This may be something as simple as the fork in a river, or something now obscured by time.

# Trow Brook

A name derived from Old English *troh*, which can still be seen in the sense of 'trough'. The name was given to describe a certain part of this watercourse which is very straight. Although at the time there was no indication that this was anything other than a natural feature, archaeology has shown this is entirely man-made. The intention may have been to divert the stream to facilitate ease of construction, yet it seems more likely to be for irrigation purposes.

# Tugford

It is sometimes possible to see an origin quite quickly. However names should never be guessed at and, even when the meaning is clear, it is vital to go through the process of examining early forms if only to check one's initial thoughts. Tugford is an example of this, for it takes little insight to see this as being of Saxon origin with a personal name followed by *ford*. Indeed this is the case, for 'Tucga's ford' is recorded as *Tuggeford* in 1138. The earlier record of *Dodefort* in 1086 can be discounted as one of Domesday's less reliable entries.

The name of **Baucott** tells us this was where we would have found 'the cottages at the rounded hill'; **The Tack** was used only as 'temporary pasture', with **The Bylet** being 'the piece of land cut off by the Tugford Mill race'.

# U

## Uffington

A name of Old English origins recorded as *Uffentun* in 936 and *Offentone* in Domesday. Here the Saxon personal name is suffixed by *tun* and is 'Uffa's farmstead'.

## Uppington

In Domesday it is *Opetone*, while a century later it has become *Oppinton*. Here are three Old English or Saxons elements, a personal name followed by *inga* and *tun* and giving us 'farmstead of the family or followers of Uppa'.

# W

## Walford

This name is recorded in Domesday as *Waleford* and is derived from the Old English *waella + ford* and telling this was '(the place) at the spring by a ford'.

## Wall

This is not what it may seem; indeed this name has different origins in Shropshire to elsewhere in England. Here the name comes from Old English *waella* thus describing this as '(the place at) the spring or stream'. There are in fact two places in the county, **East Wall** and **Wall under Heywood** listed as *Walle* in 1200 and *Walle sub Eywode* in 1255. Being less than 2 miles apart, the additions were necessary to distinguish them. The former is most certainly east of the other, where the addition comes from Old English *haege* or *hege + wudu*, 'within or near the enclosed wood'.

## Watling Street

Some may argue that a street name is not a place which merits its own entry. However this former Roman road and major trunk road is one of the longest in the country. Furthermore it is the only major road from antiquity which runs predominantly east–west rather than straight north–south.

The name of the road comes from a place name, itself from a Saxon personal name. Listed in the ninth century as *Waeclinga straet* this is a name which refers to '(the place at) the Roman road associated with the family or followers of Wacol'. The place in question is recorded as *Waeclingaceaster* around AD 900. It still exists, although today we know the place as St Albans.

Doubtless the name was soon applied to the stretch of road between St Albans and London. However it would also have been known as this in the opposite direction and the road leading to St Albans would have been the same from both sides, thus the whole 260-mile-long road was eventually known as Watling Street.

In fact there may be a place called Watling Street which could be considered to be a settlement, albeit a very small one. However, it could also be seen as one of a collection of minor names, little more than field names.

Others in this vicinity include **Wellington Hay**; the basic name has the same origins as Wellington (see the following entry) while the additional Middle English *hay* refers to a 'part of the forest fenced off specifically for hunting'. **Buckatree Hall** takes its name from a small settlement once known as 'Bucca's tree'. The basic name of Boynhale is 'Boia's nook of land', which take on *hyrne* 'corner' to give **Boynhale Hurne** and *hlidgeat* 'swing gate' in **Boynhale Lydeyate**.

# Wellington

Despite having records to hand such as *Walintone* from 1086, *Waletona* 1181, *Weliton* 1192, *Wolinton* 1196, *Welintona* 1220, and *Weolyntone* 1327, the personal name is somewhat uncertain. This is not so much because of the early listings, but rather the personal name itself.

If the Saxons had used names such as Mick, Mike, Mickey, or Mitch we would have difficulty discerning between them – indeed it would be probably be nearly impossible to state categorically that any of these were pet forms of Michael, Mitchell, Michelle or Michaela. While this is an extreme example, it does show how even the question of gender may be quite difficult to ascertain. Here the Old English personal name is followed by *inga* and *tun* giving this as 'the farmstead of the family or followers of Weola', or similar.

Local names here include **Fish Pit**, where fish remains were used as a fertiliser; **Slang**, which is 'a very narrow strip of land' and **Dothill**, 'the rounded hill'. **Haygate** is *hay geat* meaning 'the route to the fenced-off hunting forest'; **Walker Street** features a trade name *walcere* or 'fuller', a process in the making of cloth; **Clem Park**, from Old English *claeme* describing a 'muddy place' and **Hoar Stone** listed in 1741 as *dwelling house called the Hour Stone* and from Old English *har stan* speaking of 'the boundary stone'.

# Welshampton

Recorded in Domesday as simply *Hantone*, it is not until 1649 that we find the modern name as *Welch Hampton*. The basic Old English *heah + tun* tells us this was the 'high farmstead', not necessarily of greater elevation but probably in the sense of having greater stature or value.

The addition may be somewhat misleading, for there is no reason to believe the residents here were Welsh. It probably refers to a time during the seventh century when the settlement was very close to a small portion of Flintshire which had become isolated from the rest of the county. Flint, as it was usually termed, was the smallest county in Wales until its demise in the twentieth century through political and administrative boundary changes.

# Wem

Listed in Domesday as *Weme* and in 1228 as *Wemme*, this name is Old English and related to *wamm* meaning 'stain'. The actual word is unknown but, based on the knowledge we have of how languages evolve, is probably *wemm* which is used to refer to 'the dirty or muddy place'.

One of Wem's most famous residents is honoured by the name of **Eckford Park**. Named after nursery man Henry Eckford, his efforts are seen in many gardens throughout the world for it was he, in 1882, who developed the first of his many varieties of sweet pea. Indeed the popular climber should correctly be referred to as the Eckford sweet pea.

One pub here is the **Old Post Office** which was indeed the local post office until 1980, unlike the similarly named pub in Shrewsbury which was a posting stop as a former coaching house.

*The Old Post Office at Wem, now a most welcoming public house.*

# Wenlock

There are actually two places with this ancient name, **Much Wenlock** and **Little Wenlock**, and are separated by about 5 miles with the River Severn running between them. Little Wenlock is the easiest to explain for it takes its name from the other, it once being on land held by the monks of Wenlock Priory. The addition of 'Little' is simply to differentiate and should be expected. It does seem unlikely that this was the original name of Little Wenlock; however what the earlier name was is unrecorded.

The addition of 'Much' comes from Old English *mycel* and is a variation on Great, sometimes seen as Magna, a Latin variation on the same theme. Records of Wenlock go back a long way, first seen as *Wininicas* in 675, then *Wenlocan* and *Winlocan* in the ninth century, with Domesday recording it as *Wenloch*. These last three forms show the evolution of the name quite well, while also pointing out the Old English suffix of *loca* which is 'enclosed place' and most likely refers to the monastery.

There have been suggestions that the first element is a personal name, perhaps that of the saint associated with the monastery, or maybe its founder. However, that seventh-century listing has no resemblance to any known name. It is likely this is another transferred name, the original being that of **Wenlock Edge**. The 'Edge' is self-explanatory. The *Wininicas* could be Celtic *winn* 'white' and a description of the limestone rock of Wenlock.

The Edge is a region of outstanding natural beauty, a dramatic limestone escarpment of fossils and fauna of great value to the scientific community. What is less well known is the association with William Penny Brookes, whose attempted revival of the Olympic Games in the town in 1850 eventually led to the massive four-yearly spectacle we see today.

Much Wenlock has a wealth of interesting and diverse names within and around the place. **Atterley**, for example, is listed as *Atterleg* in 1225 and *Atterleye* in 1334. Clearly the suffix here is Old English *leah* or 'woodland clearing', although the first element is uncertain. The most obvious suggestion is Middle English *atter*, 'place at the'. However, this combination is unknown in place names and even if this is exceptional we should expect this to have become Natterley or even Ratterley. Without evidence of either we can discount this origin. The closest is Old English *aetter* which, depending on its usage, can either describe 'ant' or 'poison'. Perhaps here we have an indication of a woodland glade which was overgrown with nettles, for formic acid is the weapon of both the nettle and the ant.

Commonly found names include **Walton** from *waelle tun* meaning 'the settlement near a spring'. There is also **Bourton** *burh tun* or 'the fortified settlement', and **Bradeley** from *brad leah* or '(the place at) the broad woodland clearing'.

One name almost provides a history lesson in its own right. As stated under the listing for nearby Rushbury there is a place called Roman Bank, indeed there is another at Barrow. Here too is evidence that Roman artefacts were uncovered at some stage, leaving a legacy of names such as **Roman Coppice**, **Romans Rough**, **The Big Romans**, **The Little Romans**, **The Far Romans**, **The Romans Meadow** and once *The Romones* in 1597 too. Another with multiple examples has its origins in the same discoveries. The basic name comes from Old English *dinor waella* 'the coin stream' and is seen as **Dinnawell Coppice**, **Dinnawell Cote**, **Big Dinnawell**, **Little Dinnawell**, and even somewhat corrupted as **Near Dennywell**.

If we require any further evidence of Roman occupation there is the minor place name of **The Floors**, surely a reference to a paved or tessellated floor of a Roman building. The name is mirrored in two fields in nearby Acton Round but corrupted to become The Flowers. It only takes a few moments listening to the Black Country tones, which are as close to Old English as it is possible to get, to understand how 'floors' could become 'flowers'.

**Callaughton** is seen as *Kaleweton* 1224, *Calweton* 1251 and *Caloweton* 1291, which shows it to be from *calu tun* or 'the farmstead by the hill'. **Farley** is a name which always means 'woodland clearing where ferns grow', and comes from *fearn leah*. Likewise **Wyke** is found throughout the land and is from *wic* in a plural form of *wicum*, 'specialised or dairy farms'.

The Old English *spon hyll* literally means 'wood shaving hill'; however, this should be seen as being in the sense of producing something rather than a place littered with such – i.e. it was whatever created the shavings that is important, not the shavings themselves. This has produced the names **Spoonhill Hall**, **Spoonhill Wood**, **Little Spoonhill** and **Lower Spoonhill Wood**.

**Audience Meadow** is traditionally where Charles I gathered (and presumably addressed) his men on the march from Shrewsbury to Bridgnorth. Despite the popularity of this explanation it was created to fit the corruption of the true origin. Examining records shows there is are earlier field names, now lost, of *Alden* and *Auden* telling us it was where 'alder trees grew'.

**Tick Wood** sounds less attractive than its original *ticcen wudu* or 'the goats' wood', yet conversely from *wind geat* 'the windswept pass' would entice less settlers than its modern form of **The Vineyards**. **Bull Rings** everywhere are a sign of a market place, and one where livestock were bought and sold.

Almost without exception every **High Street** should be viewed as high in a sense of importance, rather than in an elevated sense. It should be noted that it was only known by this name from 1736. Prior to this it was *Spyttle Street* a reference to St John's Hospital which was here from 1267 and which also gave a name to *Spyttle Cross* around the middle of the sixteenth century. Later came **Forester Cottage Hospital**, financed by the heritage of Lady Forester after her death in 1893.

Another lost street, which was certainly here until 1897 and probably later, was **Pouke Lane**. This is a name which is normally found as Powke and is an indication that this place was once thought to be the domain of a ghost or goblin, for that is what the word *puce* is used to describe.

**Cleedon Hill** takes its name from the creatures which were seen here. From Old English *gleoda dun* this was 'the hill where kites were seen' and hopefully will be seen again. Maybe we will also one day see a windmill again at the place known as **Old Windmill**. The previous building was constructed around the beginning of the nineteenth century and was destroyed following a lightning strike some fifty years later. **Newtown** is a name applied to a new settlement, although the first thirty-nine cottages were built here in 1736 which makes it a little less 'new' than the 'old' windmill.

**Shadwell Rock** once stood alongside Shadwell Spring. The basic name speaks of this being 'the shady place', although the water source is no more. **Standhill Rock** refers to 'the hill with a stone quarry'; **Presthope** is from *preost hop* 'the valley of the priests'.

**Five Chimneys** belonged to the five cottages built here around the beginning of the nineteenth century and which stood here until they were demolished in the 1960s. **Fridays Pool** features a day of the week which was often used as an insult in former times, here a derogatory term describing poor land. **Homer** is a shortened form of a name where the second element is Old English *mor* meaning 'marsh'. However the first element is uncertain. Without further evidence we are unable to differentiate between *hol* 'a hollow', *hana* 'male birds', and the Saxon personal name Hana.

Local names in Little Wenlock include **Huntington** or 'the huntsman's hill', **Lyde Brook** from *hylde* and meaning 'the noisy stream', **Slough Brook** which is a tributary of the Lyde and is quite different for it is slow-flowing and 'a mire' from *sloh*, while the **Spinning Ford** is named to tell us there is a sharp diversion at this point in the stream where it hits a natural outcrop of rock.

# Wentnor

An Old English name recorded as *Wantenoure* in 1086, *Wontenoure* in 1200, and *Wentenour* in 1251. The suffix here is *ofer* giving us '(the place at) the flat-topped ridge associated with Wenta or Wonta'.

# Westbury

Even without Domesday's record of *Wesberie* this name would be easy to see as coming from Old English *west* + *burh*. Here is 'the western stronghold'.

# Westhope

Recorded as *Weshope* in 1086 and as *Westhope* as early as 1267, this name is from Old English *west* + *hop* and speaking of the '(place at) the western enclosed valley'.

# Weston Rhyn

As evidenced by Domesday's *Westone* this place was only known by this very common name at the time of the great census. From Old English *west* + *tun* it is clearly 'the western farmstead'.

The addition is almost obligatory. Here it refers to **Rhyn** hill less than 2 miles away and clearly visible across the valley. This is easily recognised as a Welsh name; indeed it comes from *rhyn* which means simply 'peak' or maybe simply used here to mean 'hill'.

# Whitchurch

This is a name found in a number of counties. Not surprisingly this is the '(place at) the white church'; it comes from Old English *hwit* + *cirice* and suggests it was

stone built rather than wooden, a major difference in Saxon times. The name is listed in Domesday as *Westune* 'the west farmstead', yet the modern form can be seen as early as the thirteenth century in *Whytchyrche*. This is not the first time the place was known by this name. There is an earlier record from 1199 of *Albus Monasterium*, Latin for 'the white church'.

Streets around Whitchurch include the **Bullring**, which was last used for bull baiting in 1802. The name of **Pepper Street** is found in many Roman settlements, always referring not just to that seasoning but a supplier of spices in general.

**Alport Street** was named after the family of that name who owned property in the town from around the end of the sixteenth century. **Brownlow Street** was named after Earl Brownlow who was

*St Alkmund's Church at Whitchurch.*

*The Greyhound public house at Yardington, Whitchurch.*

lord of the manor when the road was built in 1875. In the same year **Bridgewater Street** was built, named after the Earls of Bridgewater who were lords of the manor prior to the Brownlows. The Talbot family, lords of the manor prior to the Bridgewater family, gave their name to **Talbot Street** which leads in the general direction of their former home.

**George Street** and **Elizabeth Street** were named in 1937 on the occasion of the coronation of George VI and his wife, Queen Elizabeth. **Egerton Road** remembers a former rector of St Alkmund's Church; W.H. Egerton served in the post for many years. **Worthington Street** recalls Archibald Worthington, one of Whitchurch's most generous and tireless benefactors. **Thompson Drive** was named after the Revd Mr Thompson, minister and a man who served on the district council.

**Sharps Drive** was built on land owned by Richard Sharpes, a butcher who raised his own animals for slaughter. **The Chemistry** is named after a chemical works which produced products used in the tanning of leather. **Queens Road** was named such in 1897 on the occasion of the Diamond Jubilee of Queen Victoria; around the same time **Salisbury Road** was named to mark the prime minister the Marquis of Salisbury. Finally there is **Sherrymill Hill**, named after the mill on Staggs Brook and the name of a miller and where the gas works were built in more recent times.

Painter Randolph Caldecott lived and worked around the present **Caldecott Crescent** in 1865. His work was known around the world, his best-known illustrations being that of children's nursery rhymes, while published work includes those appearing in *Punch*, *The Times* and many, many children's books.

It seems odd that, for a town which styles itself 'the home of tower clocks', there are not more street names allied to this precision industry. For over three centuries clocks adorning towers have been shipped to some of the most imposing buildings around the world. Best known are the Joyce family. J.B. Joyce & Co. Ltd has led the market in the town for over two hundred years. To commemorate the new millennium the company produced the clock which stands in the Bullring; it shows examples of Whitchurch's name over the centuries. Hopefully the town's planners and developers will correct that oversight before long.

# Whitley

A small village to the north of the county with a name which is found regularly throughout England. It seems to have been given to regions near to the main settlement and always refers to 'the white wood or clearing', probably a reference to the distinct bark of silver birch found growing on the edge of the clearing.

# Whittingslow

The inclusion of 'ing' here normally points to a personal name, referring to the 'family or followers of'. Here is different, as evidenced by the records of *Witecheslawe* 1086, *Witokeslawa* 1208, and *Whitokeslowe.* In 1274 there is a possessive 's' present, it is not simply an evolutionary error. The Old English *hlaw* is preceded by a Saxon personal name, making this the 'tumulus of a man called Hwittuc'.

# Whittington

The first element here does include the 'ing' spoken about in the previous name. Listed in Domesday as *Wititone*, in 1138 as *Quitentona*, and in 1237 as *Whitinton,* this is an Old English place name which can be defined as 'the farmstead of the family or followers of Hwita'. Here the Saxon personal name is followed by the elements *inga* and *tun*.

One legend of Whittington Castle surrounds that of Sir Fulk FitzWarin, a descendant of the Peveril family who were named among the guardians of the Holy Grail in the tales of King Arthur. Several reports have been passed down suggesting that the Marian Chalice was kept in a private chapel of the castle during the thirteenth century. Several have suggested this was, in reality, the famed Grail of Arthurian legend. However it was probably the result of some rather imaginative mid-nineteenth-century historian.

*Whittington Castle, one of a chain built along the England–Wales border.*

One pub here is the **Penrhos Arms**, which seems to refer to a family coat of arms. However the sign displays sheep grazing in the fields and there is no record of a family of this name associated with the village or the inn. It is likely that the 'arms' has been added to make it sound more like a pub name, while the supposed family name was taken from the map. This features two Welsh words *pen* meaning 'headland' and *rhos* or 'moorland', it seems unlikely that there is any other explanation.

# Whixall

While the modern forms of Whixall and Whittingslow are very different, they feature the same Saxon personal name. Records of this name are found from 1086 as *Witehala*, by 1241 it was *Whitekeshal*, in 1249 *Witekshale*, and in 1327 as *Quixhal*. The suffix here is Old English *halh* and tells us of '(the place at) Hwittuc's nook of land'.

# Wigwig

A very un-English sounding place name indeed. However records such as *Wigewic* in 1086 show this is indeed Saxon. Here the suffix has been corrupted for, as shown in Domesday, the true ending is *wic*. Normally it would be found as 'wich'. However, the first element clearly influenced pronunciation and thus spelling. A name which sounds more as if it belongs in the Australian outback comes from 'Wicga's specialised farm' – invariably such are dairy farms.

*A road sign which has brought amusement to many travellers along the A4169.*

# Willey

This place has records of *Wilit* in 1086, *Wilileg* in 1199, and *Wilileia* in 1200. There is no doubt this is from the Old English *wilig + leah* and telling of the '(place at) the willow tree clearing'.

Locally we find **Bould Farm** from *botl* which means simply 'building'. Now as all places are named to be different and clearly all settlements had a building, this must have been an exceptional building. However without any records describing it, or any forms showing a second element, it seems unlikely we will ever know just what this building was or what it was used for.

**The Dean** comes from Old English *denu* meaning 'valley', which has been cut by a tributary of the Severn so small it has no official name. **Honeypot Coppice** is a common field name always describing 'sticky soil'. **The Smithies** is from Old English *smiththe*, referring to the iron bloomeries on Linley Brook. Similarly **Willey Furnace** is a name taken from company who founded the Smithies, the New Willey Co, who were here from 1757. The name was quickly transferred to **Willey Hall**, **Willey Park** and **Willey Cottages**.

# Wistanstow

A place recorded in Domesday as *Wistanestou*, showing this is an Old English suffix of *stow*. The first element is a personal name, indeed it is that of someone we actually know something of. This place is derived from 'the holy place of St Wigstan'.

To know something of the individual concerned, no matter how little, is very unusual. Wigstan was a Prince of Mercia, son of Wigmund and Aelfflaed, who is thought to have ruled Mercia for a year following the death of his father.

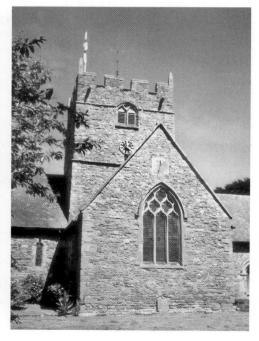

*The lych gate of the church at Wistanstow.*                *Holy Trinity Church at Wistanstow.*

The man who was to succeed him, Beorhtfrith, planned to marry his widowed mother, something Wigstan objected to vehemently. At a meeting called between them, Beofhtfrith, who is sometimes quoted as being godfather to the prince, murdered him. When Wigstan's remains were reburied in Repton, ten years after his death in 840, his tomb became a centre of pilgrimage and a cult had developed around him.

# Wistanswick

Here is a name first found in 1274 as *Wistaneswick*. Here is an Old English name with the suffix *wic* and speaking of 'Wigstan's specialised or dairy farm'. It will be noticed that there is a similarity between this and the previous name; indeed the two have identical personal names. However there is a great distance between the two and they come from two totally different eras, thus there is no way the same person was involved. However, it is possible that the name was chosen for the individual as a mark of respect for a man whose memory was greatly respected.

# Wollaston

A Saxon name recorded in Domesday as *Willavestune* and telling us this was 'Wiglaf's farmstead'.

# Wollerton

Another Saxon name yet, despite the similarity with the previous name, has a very different personal name as its first element. Early records are quite unlike those of Wollaston, this place being recorded as *Ulvretone* in 1086 and as *Wluruntona* in 1135. With the common Old English suffix *tun*, here we find 'the farmstead of a woman called Wulfrun'.

# Woodcote

A small hamlet which cannot be much larger than it was when founded centuries ago. Indeed there are few more buildings today than is revealed by the name meaning 'wood cottages'.

# Woofferton

A name not seen until 1221 as *Wulfreton*, yet it is undoubtedly a Saxon personal name with Old English *tun*. The forms are rather late for us to be completely certain of the personal name; however it would be not unlike 'the farmstead of Wulfhere or Wulffrith'.

# Woolstaston

Here is an Old English name which has undergone a change in pronunciation in comparatively recent times, probably through an error on a map, which has resulted in a name which can hardly be said to roll off the tongue! Listed in the eleventh century as *Ulestanestune* the name features a Saxon personal name combined with *tun* and tells us this was once 'Wulfstan's farmstead'.

# Worfield

Listed in Domesday as *Wrfeld*, as *Werfeld* in 1098, as *Werrefeld* in 1162, in 1174 as *Wurefeld*, *Wirefeld* in 1185 and as *Wurrefeld* in 1230. The suffix here is *feld* and tells us of the '(place at) the open land on the River Worfe'. The river name is also Old English and means simply 'winding'.

# Worthen

Despite how it appears there is only one element here, that of Old English *worthign*. Normally found as a suffix, it is unusual to find it alone but by no means unique. Listed as *Wrdine* 1086 and *Worthyn* 1246, this name simply means 'enclosure'.

# Wotherton

Domesday records this name as *Udevertune*, and only an understanding of the misunderstood forms in the eleventh-century census enables us to see this as Old English *wudu* + *ford* + *tun*. This name tells us of 'farmstead by the ford in woodland'. It must be said that this name does appear overly simplistic. In Saxon England the ford was fairly common, farms were everywhere, and woodland ubiquitous.

# Wrekin, The

A hill which has a name from the pre-Roman or British tongue. However this name was not originally applied to the hill but to the town of Wroxeter nearby and was transferred here. The name is discussed fully under the entry for Wroxeter.

On the summit of the hill are three features; **Bladder Stone**, **Raven's Bowl** and **Needle's Eye** are all named from the mythological battle between sibling rival giants Ercol and Madog. Having decided to build themselves a home they dug enough earth to create a mound (The Wrekin) and left a trench which filled with water (River Severn). Being giants meant they needed a great deal of room. Thus the Wrekin was not big enough and a squabble for dominance soon reached appropriately titanic proportions.

Ercol aimed a blow at his brother with his spade; however a passing raven attempted to intervene by pecking out his eye. The spade fell to earth and gouged out a hole now known as the Needle's Eye. A tear fell from the injured eye forming the pool known as Raven's Bowl (sometimes referred to as Cuckoo's Cup). Tradition has it that this pool has never dried out since its formation. The battle continued, the fighting so fierce that the grass still cannot gain a roothold around the Bladder's Stone.

Eventually Ercol's injury allowed his brother to gain the upper hand. Ercol was buried beneath a great mound of earth and remains there to this day, a prisoner buried beneath Ercall Hill. Some claim to have heard his cries for help, yet only when alone and on the darkest of nights.

Another legend tells of how the hill was formed by a giant by the name of Gwendol Wrekin ap Shenkin ap Mynyddmawr. For reasons unknown the giant had a grudge against Shrewsbury and decided to flood the town and kill all its inhabitants. He took his spade and dug out a huge clod of earth and set off to the west. Around Wellington he met a cobbler who had a sack full of shoes for repair, which he collected at Shrewsbury market. The giant asked for directions to Shrewsbury, revealing his plan in the process. The quick-thinking cobbler told him it was still a long way to walk, offering the worn out shoes as evidence of how many pairs he had already worn out since he had set out from the town market. The giant decided to curtail his journey and dropped the spadeful of earth where he stood, thereafter scraping his boots against the spade to clean off the mud. The large clod became the Wrekin, the smaller scrapings were to become nearby Ercall Hill.

The name has become a part of the English language, used to describe a long and circuitous route. Although the phrase is becoming less common, older members of the communities of the western Midlands counties, and in particular the Black Country, will still be heard to speak of travelling 'all around the Wrekin'.

# Wrockwardine

A name recorded as *Recordine* in 1086 and as *Wrocwurthin* in 1196. Here the suffix is the same as that found for Worthen, Old English *worthign*. This place can be defined as 'the enclosure by the hill called the Wrekin'.

One minor name from the area is **Bratton** which takes its name from 'the settlement by the brook', a brook which is a tributary of the River Tern and was called *Bullocks Brook* in 1580, is now called **Bratton Brook**, and also gave its name to **Bratton Cottage**, **Bratton Covert**, **Bratton Farm**, **Bratton Fields** and **Bratton House**.

**Burcot** comes from *bur cot* telling of 'the sleeping cottage', a literal meaning of 'bedchamber' and a likely indication of a temporary shelter, albeit a little more up-market. **Man Meadow Ford** takes its first element from Old English *maene*, 'common', the rest is self-explanatory. **Charlton** is from *ceorl tun* 'the farmstead of the serfs'; **The Flash** is from Middle English *flasshe* 'the swamp'; **Sturdy Furlong** is a name thought to signify it was 'hard to manage'.

**Cluddley**, also seen as **Clotley**, is from *clate leah* 'the woodland clearing of burdock'; **Orelton** from *eorl tun*, 'the nobleman's farmstead'; **Walcot** is 'cottages of the Britons' and a hamlet where Welsh was spoken; **Crump Meadow** comes from the Saxon for 'crooked', while **The Slade** refers to 'a patch of wet ground in the ploughed field'.

**Admaston** is 'Aethelmund's settlement', **Allscott** is 'Ealdred's cottages', **Leaton** comes from 'the farmstead in the woodland clearing', **Rushmoor** is 'the rush marsh', and **Hollandstile** 'the stile by the holly'. The names of **Grumbling Pit Leasowe**, **Lower Dumbling Hill**, **Upper Dumbling Hill** and **Tumbling Pit Leasowe** are field names which have evolved from the dialect word *dumble* meaning 'a steep hollow'.

**Tiddicross** is the name of a field and a house near a crossroads and marked as a workhouse on a sixteenth-century map. Used for charity purposes from the seventeenth century, the name refers to its charitable work.

# Wroxeter

A name recorded as early as AD 150 as *Ouirokonion*, later listed as *Rochescestre* in Domesday. This eleventh-century listing shows the suffix well-known to show a Roman settlement. However what is often mistakenly thought to be an indication that a name is of Roman or Latin origins is incorrect, this element comes from the Old English or Saxon *ceaster*. The meaning here is 'the Roman stronghold' and is clearly not a Roman name for they would have simply referred to it as 'our stronghold'.

The first element here has been transferred to the nearby hill known as the Wrekin and then to the place name of Wrockwardine. While the place has very ancient origins, and records are sparse, it is likely this place was known as *Uriconio* by the time the Romans arrived, this being derived from a Celtic term telling us it was 'the town of a man called Virico'.

# Wytheford

A name found in Domesday as *Wicford* and in 1195 as *Widiford*. The eleventh-century record can be considered erroneous; this is from Old English *withig* + *ford* and is '(the place at) the ford where will trees grow'. The name is actually found as **Great Wytheford** although there is no other place named such. Clearly there must have been a similarly named place once, the place now known by a different name or has been lost.

# Y

## Yeaton

A name listed as *Aitone* in Domesday and as *Eton* in 1327. The fourteenth-century listing is how we would normally have expected a name to have developed from the original Old English *ea* + *tun*, yet local pronunciation has clearly affected the spelling. This place began life as 'the farmstead by a river'.

## Yockleton

While Domesday records this name as *Ioclehvile*, the evolution of the suffix from *hyll* to *tun* can be seen through later listings as *Lokelthulla* in 1100, *Yokethil* in 1246, *Yokelthul* in 1274, to *Yokolton* in 1327. This is a name of Old English derivation in *geocled* + *hyll*, which began life as 'the hill by a small manor', later becoming 'the farmstead'.

Obviously this name was first applied to the hill which was referred to as being by the settlement. Later this became the farmstead by the hill of the settlement. Maybe this is suggesting that the place was abandoned for a short time, or maybe it refers to two places which were here in different eras.

## Yorton

A name recorded in Domesday as *Iartune* and derived from two Old English elements *geard* + *tun*. This is the 'farmstead with a yard'.

# Common Place Name Elements

| Element | Origin | Meaning |
|---------|--------|---------|
| *ac* | Old English | oak tree |
| *banke* | Old Scandinavian | bank, hill slope |
| *bearu* | Old English | grove, wood |
| *bekkr* | Old Scandinavian | stream |
| *berg* | Old Scandinavian | hill |
| *birce* | Old English | birch tree |
| *brad* | Old English | broad |
| *broc* | Old English | brook, stream |
| *brycg* | Old English | bridge |
| *burh* | Old English | fortified place |
| *burna* | Old English | stream |
| *by* | Old Scandinavian | farmstead |
| *ceap* | Old English | market |
| *ceaster* | Old English | Roman stronghold |
| *cirice* | Old English | church |
| *clif* | Old English | cliff, slope |
| *cocc* | Old English | woodcock |
| *cot* | Old English | cottage |
| *cumb* | Old English | valley |
| *cweorn* | Old English | queorn |
| *cyning* | Old English | king |
| *dael* | Old English | valley |
| *dalr* | Old Scandinavian | valley |
| *denu* | Old English | valley |
| *draeg* | Old English | portage |
| *dun* | Old English | hill |
| *ea* | Old English | river |

| Element | Origin | Meaning |
|---------|--------|---------|
| *east* | Old English | east |
| *ecg* | Old English | edge |
| *eg* | Old English | island |
| *eorl* | Old English | nobleman |
| *eowestre* | Old English | fold for sheep |
| *fald* | Old English | animal enclosure |
| *feld* | Old English | open land |
| *ford* | Old English | river crossing |
| *ful* | Old English | foul, dirty |
| *geard* | Old English | yard |
| *geat* | Old English | gap, pass |
| *haeg* | Old English | enclosure |
| *haeth* | Old English | heath |
| *haga* | Old English | hedged enclosure |
| *halh* | Old English | nook of land |
| *ham* | Old English | homestead |
| *hamm* | Old English | river meadow |
| *heah* | Old English | high, chief |
| *hlaw* | Old English | tumulus, mound |
| *hoh* | Old English | hill spur |
| *hop* | Old English | enclosed valley |
| *hrycg* | Old English | ridge |
| *hwaete* | Old English | wheat |
| *hwit* | Old English | white |
| *hyll* | Old English | hill |
| *lacu* | Old English | stream, watercourse |
| *lang* | Old English | long |

| Element | Origin | Meaning |
|---------|--------|---------|
| *langr* | Old Scandinavian | long |
| *leah* | Old English | woodland clearing |
| *lytel* | Old English | little |
| *meos* | Old English | moss |
| *mere* | Old English | lake |
| *middel* | Old English | middle |
| *mor* | Old English | moorland |
| *myln* | Old English | mill |
| *niwe* | Old English | new |
| *north* | Old English | north |
| *ofer* | Old English | bank, ridge |
| *pol* | Old English | pool, pond |
| *preost* | Old English | priest |
| *ruh* | Old English | rough |
| *salh* | Old English | willow |
| *sceaga* | Old English | small wood, copse |
| *sceap* | Old English | sheep |
| *stan* | Old English | stone, boundary stone |
| *steinn* | Old Scandinavian | stone, boundary stone |

| Element | Origin | Meaning |
|---------|--------|---------|
| *stapol* | Old English | post, pillar |
| *stoc* | Old English | secondary or special settlement |
| *stocc* | Old English | stump, log |
| *stow* | Old English | assembly or holy place |
| *straet* | Old English | Roman road |
| *suth* | Old English | south |
| *thorp* | Old Scandinavian | outlying farmstead |
| *treow* | Old English | tree, post |
| *tun* | Old English | farmstead |
| *wald* | Old English | woodland, forest |
| *wella* | Old English | spring, stream |
| *west* | Old English | west |
| *wic* | Old English | specialised, usually dairy farm |
| *withig* | Old English | willow tree |
| *worth* | Old English | an enclosure |
| *wudu* | Old English | wood |